How to Talk So Teens Will Listen
& Listen So Teens Will Talk

Parents will discover:

- How to express their irritation or anger without being hurtful

- Ways to respond helpfully to their teenagers' concerns

- Skills that encourage a teen to cooperate and assume responsibility

- Alternatives to punishment that help teens face their misbehaviors and make amends

- How to resolve conflicts peacefully

- How to take advantage of small opportunities to talk about sex and drugs

Teens will discover:

- What other kids their age have to say about their worries and frustrations

- Specific skills for getting along better with friends and family

- Respectful ways to voice their disagreements to their parents

John Mazlish

John Mazlish

Internationally acclaimed experts on communication between adults and children, **Adele Faber** and **Elaine Mazlish** have produced a body of work that has won the gratitude of parents and the enthusiastic praise of the professional community.

Their first book, *Liberated Parents, Liberated Children,* received the Christopher Award for "literary achievement affirming the highest values of the human spirit." Their subsequent books, *How to Talk So Kids Will Listen & Listen So Kids Will Talk* and *Siblings Without Rivalry* (#1 on the *New York Times* bestseller list) have sold more than three million copies and have translated into more than twenty languages. Their book *How to Talk So Kids Can Learn—At Home and in School* was cited by *Child* magazine as "the best book of the year for excellence in family issues in education." The authors' group workshop programs and videos produced by PBS are currently being used by parent and teacher groups around the world to improve relationships with children. Their most recent book, *How to Talk So Teens Will Listen & Listen So Teens Will Talk,* tackles the tough problems of the teenage years.

Both authors studied with the late child psychologist Dr. Haim Ginott, and are former members of the faculty of The New School for Social Research in New York and The Family Life Institute of Long Island University. In addition to their frequent lectures throughout the United States, Canada, and abroad, they have appeared on every major television talk show from *Oprah* to *Good Morning America.* They currently reside in Long Island, New York, and each is the parent of three children.

An Imprint of HarperCollinsPublishers

How to Talk So Teens Will Listen

& Listen So Teens Will Talk

Adele Faber and Elaine Mazlish

Illustrations by Kimberly Ann Coe

A hardcover edition of this book was published in 2005.
First trade paperback edition published 2006.

HarperCollins books may be purchased for educational, business, or sales
promotional use. For information please write: Special Markets Department,
HarperCollins Publishers, 10 East 53rd St, New York, NY 10022.

Library of Congress Cataloging-in-Publication Data is available

ISBN-10: 0-06-074126-0   ISBN-13: 978-0-06-074126-6

06 07 08 09 RRD 10 9 8 7 6 5 4 3 2 1

34463959   9/06

As parents, our need is to be needed; as teenagers their need is not to need us. This conflict is real; we experience it daily as we help those we love become independent of us.

—DR. HAIM G. GINOTT,
Between Parent and Teenager
(THE MACMILLAN COMPANY, 1969)

Contents

We'd Like to Thank . . .

Our families and friends, for their patience and understanding during the long writing process and for being nice enough not to ask, "So when exactly do you think you'll be finished?"

The parents in our workshops, for their willingness to try new ways of communicating with their families and for reporting their experiences back to the group. The stories they shared were an inspiration to us and to one another.

The teenagers we worked with, for everything they told us about themselves and their world. Their honest input gave us invaluable insights into their concerns.

Kimberly Ann Coe, our amazing artist, for taking all our stick figures and the words we put in their mouths and transforming them into a wonderfully varied cast of characters who bring the words to life.

Bob Markel, our literary agent and dear friend, for his enthusiasm for our project from the very beginning and for his unwavering support as we worked our way through the endless drafts that shaped this book.

Jennifer Brehl, our editor. Like the "perfect parent," she believed in us, affirmed our best, and respectfully pointed out where we might make "good" even better. She was right—every time.

Dr. Haim Ginott, our mentor. The world has changed dramatically since his passing, but his conviction that "to reach humane goals we need humane methods" remains forever true.

How This Book Came to Be

The need was there, but for a long time we didn't see it. Then letters like this began to arrive:

Dear Adele and Elaine,

HELP! When my kids were little, How to Talk . . . *was my Bible. But they're eleven and fourteen now, and I find myself facing a whole new set of problems. Have you thought about writing a book for parents of teenagers?*

Soon after there was a phone call:

"Our civic association is planning its annual Family Day Conference and we were hoping you'd be willing to give the keynote address on how to deal with teenagers."

We hesitated. We had never presented a program that focused exclusively on teenagers before. Yet the idea intrigued us. Why not? We could give an overview of the basic principles of effective communication, only this time we'd use teenage examples and demonstrate the skills by role-playing with one another.

It's always a challenge to present new material. You can never be sure if the audience will connect with it. But they did. People listened intently and responded enthusiastically. During the question-and-answer period they asked our views on everything from curfews and cliques to back talk and grounding. Afterward we were surrounded by a small group of parents who wanted to talk to us privately.

"I'm a single mom, and my thirteen-year-old son has started hanging out with some of the worst kids in the school. They're into drugs and who knows what else. I keep telling him to stay away from them, but he won't listen. I feel as if I'm fighting a losing battle. How do I get through to him?"

"I am so upset. I saw an e-mail my eleven-year-old daughter received from a boy in her class: 'I want to sex you. I want to put my dinky in your cha-cha.' I don't know what to do. Should I call his parents? Should I report it to the school? What should I say to her?"

"I've just found out my twelve-year-old is smoking pot. How do I confront her?"

"I'm scared to death. I was cleaning up my son's room and found a poem he wrote about suicide. He's doing well in school. He has friends. He doesn't seem unhappy. But maybe there's something I'm not seeing. Should I let him know I found his poem?"

"My daughter has been spending a lot of time online lately with this sixteen-year-old boy. At least, he says he's sixteen, but who knows? Now he wants to meet her. I think I should go with her. What do you think?"

On the car ride home we talked nonstop: Look at what these parents are up against! . . . What a different world we live in today! . . . But have times really changed that much? Didn't we and our friends worry about sex and drugs and peer pressure and, yes, even suicide when our kids were going through their adolescence? But somehow what we had heard tonight seemed worse, scarier. There was even more to worry about. And the problems were starting earlier. Maybe because puberty was starting earlier.

———

A few days later there was another phone call, this time from a school principal:

"We're currently running an experimental program for a group of students in both our middle school and high school. We've given a copy of How to Talk So Kids Will Listen *to each of the parents in the program. Because your book has been so helpful, we were wondering if you'd be willing to meet with the parents and conduct a few workshops for them."*

We told the principal we'd give it some thought and get back to her.

———

Over the next few days we reminisced with each other about the teenagers we once knew best—our own. We turned back time and summoned up memories of our children's adolescent years that we had long since locked away—the dark moments, the bright spots, and the times we held our breath. Little by little, we reentered the emotional terrain of yesteryear and reexperienced the same anxieties. Once again we pondered what made this stage of life so difficult.

It wasn't as if we hadn't been warned. From the time our kids were born we heard, "Enjoy them now while they're still small" . . . "Little children, little problems; big children, big problems." Over and over again we were told that one day this sweet child of ours would turn into a sullen stranger who would criticize our taste, challenge our rules, and reject our values.

So even though we were somewhat prepared for changes in our children's behavior, no one prepared us for our feelings of loss.

Loss of the old, close relationship. *(Who is this hostile person living in my home?)*

Loss of confidence. *(Why is he acting this way? Is it something I've done . . . or haven't done?)*

Loss of the satisfaction of being needed. *("No, you don't have to come. My friends will go with me.")*

Loss of the sense of ourselves as all-powerful protectors who could keep our children safe from harm. *(It's past midnight. Where is she? What is she doing? Why isn't she home yet?)*

And even greater than our sense of loss was our fear. *(How do we get our kids through these difficult years? How do we get ourselves through?)*

If that was the way it was for us a generation ago, what must it be like for mothers and fathers today? They're raising their kids in a culture that is meaner, ruder, cruder, more materialistic, more sexualized, more violent than ever before. Why wouldn't today's parents feel overwhelmed? Why wouldn't they be driven to extremes?

It's not hard to understand why some react by getting tough—why they lay down the law, punish any transgression, however minor, and keep their teens on a short leash. We can also understand why others would give up, why they'd throw up their hands, look the other way, and hope for the best. Yet both of these approaches—"Do as I say" or "Do what you want"— cut off the possibility of communication.

Why would any young person be open with a parent who is punitive? Why would he seek guidance from a parent who is permissive? Yet our teenagers' well-being—sometimes their very safety—lies in having access to the thoughts and values of their parents. Teenagers need to be able to express their doubts, confide their fears, and explore options with a grown-up who will listen to them nonjudgmentally and help them make responsible decisions.

Who, other than Mom and/or Dad, will be there for them day in, day out, through those critical years to help them counter the seductive messages of the media? Who will help them resist the pressure of their peers? Who will help them cope with the cliques and cruelties, the longing for acceptance, the fear of rejection, the terrors, excitement, and confusion of adolescence? Who will help them struggle with the push to conform and the pull to be true to themselves?

Living with teenagers can be overwhelming. We know. We remember. But we also remember how we hung on during those turbulent years to the skills we had learned and how they helped us navigate the roughest waters without going under.

Now it was time to pass on to others what had been so meaningful to us. And to learn from this current generation what would be meaningful to them.

We called the principal and scheduled our first workshop for parents of teenagers.

Authors' Note

This book is based on the many workshops we've given around the country and those we've run for parents and teenagers, separately and together, in New York and Long Island. To tell our story as simply as possible, we condensed our many groups into one and combined the two of us into one leader. Though we have changed names and rearranged events, we have been faithful to the essential truth of our experience.

—Adele Faber and Elaine Mazlish

One

Dealing with Feelings

I didn't know what to expect.

As I ran from the parking lot to the school entrance, I held on tightly to my blowing umbrella and wondered why anyone would leave a warm home on such a cold, miserable night to come to a workshop on teenagers.

The head of the guidance department greeted me at the door and ushered me into a classroom where roughly twenty parents sat waiting.

I introduced myself, congratulated them all for braving the bad weather, and distributed name tags for everyone to fill out. As they wrote and chatted with one another, I had a chance to study the group. It was diverse—almost as many men as women, different ethnic backgrounds, some couples, some alone, some in professional attire, some in jeans.

When everyone seemed ready, I asked people to introduce themselves and tell us a little about their children.

There was no hesitation. One after the other, parents described kids who ranged in age from twelve to sixteen. Almost everyone commented on the difficulty of coping with teenagers in today's world. Still, it seemed to me people were being guarded, holding back, making sure they didn't disclose too much too soon to a room full of strangers.

"Before we go any further," I said, "I want to assure you that anything we discuss here will be confidential. Whatever is said within these four walls remains here. It's no one else's business whose kid is smoking, drinking, playing hooky, or having sex a lot earlier than we'd wish. Can we all agree to that?"

Heads nodded in assent.

"I see us as partners in an exciting venture," I went on. "My job will be to present methods of communication that can lead to more satisfying relationships between parents and teenagers. Your job will be to test these methods—to put them into action in your home and report back to the group. What was or wasn't helpful? What did or didn't work? By joining forces, we'll determine the most effective ways to help our kids make that tough transition from childhood to adulthood."

I paused here for the group's reaction. "Why does it have to be a 'tough transition'?" a father protested. "I don't remember having such a hard time when I was a teenager. And I don't remember giving my parents a hard time."

"That's because you were an easy kid," said his wife, grinning and patting his arm.

"Yeah, well maybe it was easier to be 'easy' when we were teenagers," another man commented. "There's stuff going on today that was unheard of back then."

"Suppose we all go back to 'back then'," I said. "I think there are things we can learn from our own adolescence that might give us some insight into what our kids are experiencing today. Let's start by trying to remember what was best about that time in our lives."

Michael, the man who had been the "easy kid," spoke first. "The best part for me was sports and hanging out with friends."

Someone else said, "For me it was the freedom to come and go. Getting on a subway by myself. Going to the city. Getting on a bus and going to the beach. Total fun!"

Others chimed in. "Being allowed to wear high heels and makeup and that whole excitement over boys. Me and my girlfriends would have a crush on the same guy, and it was, 'Do you think he likes me or do you think he likes you?'"

"Life was so easy then. I could sleep till noon on weekends. No worries about getting a job, paying the rent, supporting a family. And no worries about tomorrow. I knew I could always count on my parents."

"For me it was a time to explore who I was and experiment with different identities and dream about the future. I was free to fantasize, but I also had the safety of my family."

One woman shook her head. "For me," she said ruefully, "the best part of adolescence was growing out of it."

I looked at her name tag. "Karen," I said, "it sounds as if that wasn't the greatest time in your life."

"Actually," she said, "it was a relief to be done with it."

"Done with what?" someone asked.

Karen shrugged before answering. "Done with worrying about being accepted . . . and trying too hard . . . and smiling too hard so people would like me . . . and never really fitting in . . . always feeling like an outsider."

Others quickly built upon her theme, including some who only moments before had spoken glowingly of their teen years:

"I can relate to that. I remember feeling so awkward and insecure. I was overweight back then and hated the way I looked."

"I know I mentioned my excitement over boys, but the truth is, it was more like an obsession—liking them, breaking up with them, losing friends because of them. Boys were all I ever thought about, and my grades showed it. I almost didn't graduate."

"My problem in those days was the pressure I was under from the other guys to do stuff I knew was wrong or dangerous. I did a lot of stupid things."

"I remember always feeling confused. Who am I? What are my likes? My dislikes? Am I true or am I a copycat? Can I be my own person and still be accepted?"

I liked this group. I appreciated their honesty. "Tell me," I asked, "during those roller-coaster years, was there anything your parents said or did that was helpful to you?"

People searched their memories.

"My parents never yelled at me in front of my friends. If I did something wrong, like coming home really late, and my friends were with me, my parents waited until they were gone. Then they'd let me have it."

"My father used to say things to me like, 'Jim, you have to stand up for your beliefs . . . When in doubt, consult your conscience . . . Never be afraid to be wrong or you'll never be right.' I used to think, 'There he goes again,' but sometimes I really did hang on to his words."

"My mother was always pushing me to improve. 'You can do better . . . Check it again . . . Do it over.' She didn't let me get away with anything. My father, on the other hand, thought I was perfect. So I knew who to go to for what. I had a good mix."

"My parents insisted I learn all kinds of different skills— how to balance a checkbook, change a tire. They even made me read five pages of Spanish a day. I resented it then, but ended up getting a good job because I knew Spanish."

"I know I shouldn't be saying this, because there are probably a lot of working mothers here, including me, but I really liked having my mother there when I got home from school. If anything upsetting happened to me during the day, I could always tell her about it."

"So," I said, "many of you experienced your parents as being very supportive during your adolescent years."

"That's only half the picture," Jim said. "Along with my father's positive sayings, there was plenty of stuff that hurt. Nothing I did was ever good enough for him. And he let me know it."

Jim's words opened the floodgates. Out poured a torrent of unhappy memories:

"I got very little support from my mother. I had a lot of problems and needed guidance badly, but all I ever got from her were the same old stories: 'When I was your age . . . ' After a while I learned to keep everything inside."

"My parents used to lay these guilt trips on me: 'You're our only son . . . We expect more from you . . . You're not living up to your potential.' "

"My parents' needs always came before mine. They made their problems my problems. I was the oldest of six and was expected to cook and clean and take care of my brothers and sisters. I had no time to be a teenager."

"I had the opposite. I was so babied and overprotected, I didn't feel capable of making any decisions without my parents' approval. It took years of therapy for me to begin to have some confidence in myself."

"My parents were from another country—a whole other culture. In my house everything was strictly prohibited. I couldn't buy what I wanted, couldn't go where I wanted, couldn't wear what I wanted. Even when I was a senior in high school, I had to ask permission for everything."

A woman named Laura was the last to speak.

"My mother went to the other extreme. She was far too lenient. She didn't enforce any rules. I came and went as I pleased. I could stay out till two or three in the morning and nobody cared. There was never a curfew or any kind of intervention. She even let me get high in the house. At sixteen, I was doing coke and drinking. The scary part was how fast I went downhill. I still experience anger at my mother for not even trying to give me structure. She destroyed many years of my life."

The group was silent. People were feeling the impact of what they had just heard. Finally Jim commented, "Boy, parents may mean well, but they can really mess a kid up."

"But we all survived," Michael protested. "We grew up, got married, started families of our own. One way or another, we managed to become functioning adults."

"That may be true," said Joan, the woman who had referred to her therapy, "but too much time and energy went into getting past the bad stuff."

"And there are some things you never get past," Laura added. "That's why I'm here. My daughter is beginning to act out in ways that worry me, and I don't want to repeat with her what my mother did to me."

Laura's comment propelled the group into the present. Little by little, people began to voice their current anxieties about their children:

"What concerns me is my son's new attitude. He doesn't want to live by anyone's rules. He's a rebel. Same as I was at fifteen. But I hid it. He's out in the open. Insists on pushing the envelope."

"My daughter is only twelve, but her ego craves acceptance— especially from boys. I'm afraid that one day she'll put herself in a compromising position, just to be popular."

"I worry about my son's schoolwork. He's not applying himself anymore. I don't know if he's too into sports or just being lazy."

"All my son seems to care about now are his new friends and being cool. I don't like him hanging out with them. I think they're a bad influence."

"My daughter is like two different people. Outside the house she's a doll—sweet, pleasant, polite. But at home, forget it. The minute I tell her she can't do something or have something, she gets nasty."

"Sounds like my daughter. Only the one she gets nasty with is her new stepmother. It's a very tense situation—especially when we're all together for the weekend."

"I worry about the whole teen scene. Kids these days don't know what they're smoking or drinking. I've heard too many stories about parties where guys slip drugs into a girl's drink and about date rape."

The air was heavy with the group's collective anxiety.

Karen laughed nervously. "Well now that we know what the problems are—quick, we need some answers!"

"There are no quick answers," I said. "Not with teenagers. You can't protect them from all the dangers in today's world, or spare them the emotional turmoil of their adolescent years, or get rid of a pop culture that bombards them with unwhole-some messages. But if you can create the kind of climate in your home where your kids feel free to express their feelings, there's a good chance they'll be more open to hearing your feel-ings. More willing to consider your adult perspective. More able to accept your restraints. More likely to be protected by your values."

"You mean there's still hope!" Laura exclaimed. "It's not too late? Last week I woke up with this terrible feeling of panic. All I could think was that my daughter wasn't a little girl anymore and there was no going back. I lay there paralyzed and thought about all the things I did wrong with her, and then I felt so de-pressed and so guilty.

"Then it hit me. Hey, I'm not dead yet. She's not out of the house yet. And I'm always going to be her mother. Maybe I can learn to be a better mother. Please, tell me it's not too late."

"It's been my experience," I assured her, "that it's never too late to improve a relationship with a child."

"Really?"

"Really."

It was time to start the first exercise.

———

"Pretend I'm your teenager," I said to the group. "I'm going to tell you a few things that are on my mind and ask you to respond in a way that's guaranteed to turn most kids off. Here we go:

"I don't know if I want to go to college."

My "parents" jumped right in:

"Don't be ridiculous. Of course you're going to college."

"That is the dumbest thing I've ever heard."

"I can't believe you would even say that. Do you want to break your grandparents' heart?"

Everyone laughed. I continued airing my worries and grievances:

"Why do I always have to be the one to take out the garbage?"

"Because you never do anything else around here except eat and sleep."

"Why do you always have to be the one to complain?"

"How come your brother doesn't give me a hard time when I ask him for help?"

"We had this long lecture on drugs today from a policeman. What a crock! All he did was try to scare us."

"Scare you? He's trying to knock some sense into your head."

"If I ever catch you using drugs, you'll really have something to be scared of."

"The trouble with you kids today is that you think you know everything. Well, let me tell you, you've got a lot to learn."

"I don't care if I've got a fever. No way am I missing that concert!"

"That's what you think. You're not going anywhere tonight—except bed."

"Why would you want to do anything that stupid? You're still sick."

"It's not the end of the world. There'll be plenty of other concerts. Why don't you play the band's latest album, close your eyes, and pretend you're at the concert."

Michael snorted, "Oh yeah, that oughta go over real big!"

"Actually," I said, "as your child, nothing I heard just now went over 'real big' with me. You dismissed my feelings, ridiculed my thoughts, criticized my judgment, and gave me unsolicited advice. And you did it all so easily. How come?"

"Because it's what's in our heads," Laura said. "It's what we heard when we were kids. It's what comes naturally."

"I also think it's natural," I said, "for parents to push away painful or upsetting feelings. It's hard for us to listen to our teenagers express their confusion or resentment or disappointment or discouragement. We can't bear to see them unhappy. So it's with the best of intentions that we dismiss their feelings and impose our adult logic. We want to show them the 'right' way to feel.

"And yet, it's our listening that can give the greatest comfort. It's our acceptance of their unhappy feelings that can make it easier for our kids to cope with them."

"Oh boy!" Jim exclaimed. "If my wife were here tonight, she'd say, 'See, that's what I've been trying to tell you. Don't give me logic. Don't ask all those questions. Don't tell me what I did wrong or what I should do next time. Just *listen!*' "

"You know what I realize?" Karen said. "Most of the time I *do* listen—to everyone except my kids. If one of my friends were upset, I wouldn't dream of telling her what to do. But with my kids it's a whole other story. I move right in. Maybe it's because I'm listening to them as a parent. And as a parent, I feel I have to fix things.' "

"That's the big challenge," I said. "To shift our thinking from 'how do *I* fix things?' to 'how do I enable my kids to fix things for themselves?' "

I reached into my briefcase and handed out the illustrations I had prepared for this first meeting. "Here," I said, "in cartoon form are some basic principles and skills that can be helpful to our teenagers when they're troubled or upset. In each case you'll see the contrast between the kind of talk that can add to their distress and the kind that can help them to deal with it. There are no guarantees that our words will produce the positive outcomes you see here, but at the very least they do no damage."

Instead of Dismissing Feelings . . .

Mom doesn't want Abby to feel bad. But by dismissing her
daughter's distress, she unwittingly adds to it.

Identify Thoughts and Feelings

Mom can't take away all of Abby's pain, but by putting her
thoughts and feelings into words, she helps her daughter
deal with reality and gather the courage to move on.

Instead of Ignoring Feelings . . .

Mom has good intentions. She wants her son to do well in school. But by criticizing his behavior, dismissing his worry, and telling him what to do, she makes it harder for him to tell himself what to do.

Acknowledge Feelings with a Word or Sound
(Oh . . . mmm . . . uh . . . I see.)

Mom's minimal, empathic responses help her son feel understood and free him to focus on what he needs to do.

Instead of Logic and Explanations . . .

When Dad responds to his daughter's unreasonable request with a reasonable explanation, she becomes even more frustrated.

Give in Fantasy What You Can't Give in Reality

By giving his daughter what she wants in fantasy, Dad makes it a little easier for her to accept reality.

Instead of Going Against
Your Better Judgment . . .

In order to make her son happy and avoid a battle,
Mom ignores her better judgment and takes the
path of least resistance.

Accept Feelings as You Redirect Unacceptable Behavior

By showing empathy for her son's predicament, Mom makes it a little easier for him to accept her firm limits.

The comments began even before everyone had finished reading.

"You must've been in my house! Everything you shouldn't say sounds exactly like me."

"What bothers me is that all these scenarios have such happy endings. My kids would never give up or give in that easily."

"But this isn't about getting kids to give up or give in. It's about trying to really hear what they're feeling."

"Yeah, but to do that, you have to listen in a different way."

"And speak in a different way. It's like learning a whole new language."

"And to become comfortable with a new language," I said, "to make it your own, it helps to practice. Let's start now. Suppose I play your teenager again. I'll express my same concerns, only this time, Mom and Dad, you'll react by using any one of the skills you've just seen illustrated."

People immediately started thumbing through their pages of cartoons. I gave them a moment before launching into my list of worries. Some of the group's responses to me came quickly; others took time. People started, stopped, rephrased, and finally found the words that satisfied them.

"I don't know if I want to go to college."
"Sounds as if you're having some real doubts about it."
"You're wondering if college is right for you."
"Know what would be cool? If you could look into a crystal ball and see what your life would be like if you didn't go to college . . . or if you did."

"Why do I always have to be the one to take out the garbage?"
"Boy, I hear how much you resent it."

"It's not your favorite activity. Tomorrow let's talk about rotating chores. Right now I need your help."

"Wouldn't it be great if the garbage would take itself out?"

"We had this long lecture on drugs today from a policeman. What a crock! All he did was try to scare us."

"So you think he was exaggerating—trying to frighten kids into staying away from drugs."

"Scare tactics really turn you off."

"Sounds as if you wish adults would give kids straight information and trust them to make responsible decisions."

"I don't care if I've got a fever. No way am I missing that concert!"

"What rotten luck to be sick—on today of all days! You've been looking forward to that concert for weeks."

"I know. You had your heart set on going. The problem is, with a fever of 101, you belong in bed."

"Even though you know there will be plenty of other concerts, you sure wish you didn't have to miss this one."

When the exercise finally came to an end, people looked pleased with themselves. "I think I'm beginning to get it," Laura called out. "The idea is to try to put into words what you think the kid is feeling, but hold back on what *you're* feeling."

"Now that's the one part I object to," Jim said. "When do I get to talk about *my* feelings—to say what *I* want to say? For instance: 'Doing chores is a contribution to family life.' 'Going to college is a privilege; it can change your life.' 'Doing drugs is dumb; it can ruin your life.' "

"Yeah," Michael agreed, "after all, we're the parents. When do we get to talk about what *we* believe or what *we* value?"

"There will always be time for you to get your message across," I said, "but you have a better chance of being heard if you start by letting your kids know they've been heard. Even then there are no guarantees. They may accuse you of not understanding, of being unreasonable or old-fashioned. But make no mistake. Despite their put-downs and protests, your teenagers want to know exactly where you stand. Your values and beliefs play a vital role in determining their choices."

I took a deep breath. We had covered a lot of ground this evening. It was time for the parents to go home and test what they had learned. Up till now, they had been riding on the strength of my convictions. Only by putting the skills into action with their own teenagers and observing the results for themselves could they develop their own convictions.

"See you next week," I said. "I look forward to hearing about your experiences."

The Stories

I didn't know what would come of our first meeting. It's one thing to try to apply new principles to hypothetical problems when you're sitting around with other parents in a workshop. It's quite another when you're all alone at home, trying to cope with real kids and real problems. And yet, many of the parents did just that. Here, with slight editing, is a sampling of their experiences. (You'll notice that most of the stories come from the same people who participated actively in class. However, some come from parents who seldom joined the discussion but who wanted to share—in writing—how their new skills had affected their relationships with their teenagers.)

Joan

My daughter Rachel has seemed down in the dumps lately. But any time I'd ask her to tell me what was wrong, she'd say, "Nothing." I'd say, "How can I help you if you won't tell me?" She'd say, "I don't want to talk about it." I'd say, "Maybe if you talk about it, you'd feel better." Then she'd throw me a look and that ended that.

But after our discussion in class last week, I decided to try the "new approach." I said, "Rachel, you seem so unhappy lately. Whatever it is, something is making you feel really bad."

Well, the tears started rolling down her cheeks, and little by little the whole story came out. The two girls who had been her friends all through grade school and middle school were now part of the new popular crowd, and they were freezing her out. They didn't save a seat for her at lunch the way they used to, or invite her to any of their parties. They hardly even said hello to her anymore when they passed her in the hall. And she was positive it was one of them who sent an e-mail to some other kids about how the "dorky" clothes she wears make her look fat and don't even have brand names.

I was shocked. I had heard that this kind of thing went on in school, and I knew how cruel some girls could be, but I never imagined that anything like this would ever happen to my daughter.

All I wanted to do was take away her pain. Tell her to forget about those nasty, rotten girls. She'd make new friends. Better friends. Friends who would appreciate what a great kid she is. But I didn't say anything like that. Instead, I just talked about her feelings. I said, "Oh honey, that's rough. To find out that the people you trusted and thought were friends aren't really your friends has got to hurt."

"How could they be so mean!" she said and cried some more. Then she told me about another girl in her class they were "dissing" online—saying she had body odor and smelled of pee.

I could hardly believe what I was hearing. I told Rachel that this sort of behavior says everything about the kind of people they are and nothing about anybody else. Evidently the only way these girls can feel special, part of the "in-group," is to make sure everyone else is kept out.

She nodded her head, and we talked for a long time after that—about "true" friends and "false" friends and how to tell the difference. After a while I could see that she was starting to feel a little better.

But I couldn't say the same for myself. So the next day, after Rachel left for school, I contacted her guidance counselor. I told her that the call was confidential, but that I thought she might want to know what was going on.

I had no idea what kind of response I'd get, but she was great. She said she was very glad I had called because she had been hearing more and more stories lately about what she referred to as "cyber bullying" and that she had been planning to discuss the problem with the principal to see what could be done to help all the students understand how damaging this kind of online abuse and harassment can be.

By the end of our conversation I felt a whole lot better. I actually found myself thinking, *Who knows? Maybe something good will come of all this.*

Jim

My oldest son has a part-time job at a fast-food restaurant. Last Saturday, when he came home from work, he slammed his backpack on the table and began cursing out his boss. Every other word out of his mouth started with an *f* or an *s*.

It turns out that when his boss had asked him if he'd put in some extra hours on weekends, my son told him, "Maybe." But when he got to work on Saturday morning and was about to tell the boss he'd definitely do it, the "bastard" (to quote my son) had given away the overtime to someone else.

Well, the kid was lucky I didn't let loose with what I really wanted to say: "Why does that surprise you? What did you expect? Grow up! How's a man supposed to run a business with an employee who tells him 'maybe' he'll work. 'Maybe' doesn't cut it."

But I didn't chew him out. And I didn't even mention the cursing—this time. I just said, "So you didn't feel you had to give him a definite answer right away." He said, "No, I needed to think about it!"

I said, "Uh-huh."

He said, "I've got a life besides this job, you know!"

I thought, *This stuff isn't working.*

Then from out of the blue he says, "I guess I goofed. I should've called him when I got home and not left him hanging."

How about that? I showed him a little understanding, and he owned up to what he should've done in the first place!

Laura

A few days after our workshop I took my daughter shopping for jeans. Big mistake. Nothing she tried on was "right." It wasn't the right fit, or the right color, or the right designer label. Finally she found a pair she liked—a low-cut, skintight number that she could barely zip up and that outlined every part of her bottom.

I didn't say a word. I just left her in the dressing room and went out to look for a larger size. When I came back, she was still admiring herself in the mirror. She took one look at the pants I held up for her and started yelling, "I'm not trying those on! You want me to look like a nerd! Just because you're fat, you think everyone should wear big clothes. Well, I'm not gonna hide my body the way you do!"

I was so hurt, so angry, I came very close to calling her a little bitch. But I didn't. I said, "I'll wait for you outside." It was all I could manage.

She said, "What about my jeans?"

I repeated, "I'll wait for you outside," and left her in the dressing room.

When she finally came out, the last thing I wanted to do was "acknowledge her feelings," but I did anyway. I said, "I know you liked those jeans. And I know you're upset because I don't approve of them." Then I let her know how I felt. "When I'm spoken to that way, something in me shuts down. I don't feel like shopping anymore, or helping anymore, or even talking anymore."

Neither one of us said anything on the whole ride home. But just before we got to the house, she mumbled, "Sorry."

It wasn't much of an apology, but still, I was glad to hear it. I was also glad I hadn't said anything to her that I would've had to apologize for.

Linda

I don't know if my relationship with my son is any better, but I think I'm making some headway with his friends. They're thirteen-year-old twins, Nick and Justin, both very bright, but out of control. They smoke (I suspect more than cigarettes), they hitch rides, and once when their parents grounded them, they climbed out their bedroom window and went to the mall.

My son is flattered by their interest in him, but I'm worried. I'm sure he's been hitching rides with them, even though he denies it. If I had my way, I'd forbid him to see them outside of school. But my husband says that would only make things worse, that he'll find a way to see them anyway and lie about it.

So our strategy over the past month has been to invite the twins over for dinner every Saturday. We figure that if they're here, we can keep an eye on all of them and drive them to where they want to go. At least for one night we'd know they weren't standing on a dark corner somewhere with their thumbs out, waiting for some stranger in a car to pick them up.

Anyway, what all this is leading up to is that until now we could never get a conversation going with either of the twins. But after last week's workshop we actually made some progress.

The two of them were bad-mouthing their science teacher and calling him a stupid jerk. Normally we would've defended the teacher. But not this time. This time we tried to acknowledge how the twins felt about him. My husband said, "This is one teacher you really don't like." And they kept telling us more: "He's so boring. And he always yells at you for no reason. And if he calls on you and you don't know the answer, he puts you down in front of everybody."

I said, "Nick, I'll bet if you and Justin were teachers, you wouldn't yell at kids or put them down for not knowing an answer."

They both said, "Right!" at almost the same time.

My husband added, "And neither one of you would be boring. Kids would be lucky to have you two as their teachers."

They looked at each other and laughed. My son sat there with his mouth open. He couldn't believe his "cool" friends were actually having a conversation with his "uncool" parents.

Karen

Last night Stacey and I were looking through an old photograph album. I pointed to a picture of her on her bicycle when she was about six and said, "Look how cute you were!"

"Yeah," she said, *"then."* I said, "What do you mean *'then'*?" She said, "I don't look that good now." I said, "Don't be silly. You look fine." She said, "No, I don't. I look gross. My hair's too short, my boobs are too small, and my butt's too big."

It always gets to me when she talks that way about herself. It reminds me of my own insecurities when I was her age and how my mother was always at me with suggestions for how I could improve myself: "Don't slouch . . . Hold your shoulders up . . . Do something with your hair . . . Put a little makeup on. You look like the wrath of God!"

So yesterday when Stacey started picking herself apart, my first instinct was to reassure her: "There's absolutely nothing wrong with your butt, your hair will grow, and so will your breasts. And if they don't, you can always pad your bra."

Well, that's the kind of thing I *would've* said. But this time I thought, *Okay, I'll go with her feelings.* I put my arm around her and said, "You don't sound at all satisfied with the way you look. . . . You know what I wish? I wish that the next time you stand in front of a mirror that you'd be able to see what I see."

She suddenly looked interested. "What do you see?"

I told her the truth. "I see a girl who's beautiful—inside and out."

She said, "Oh, you're my mother," and left the room.

A minute later I saw her posing in front of the full-length mirror in the hall. She had her hand on her hip and she was actually smiling at herself.

Michael

Remember I mentioned my son's negative attitude toward school? Well, the morning after our workshop he came down to breakfast in his usual bad mood. He was stomping around the kitchen, complaining about all the pressure he was under. He had to take two big tests—Spanish and geometry—in one day.

I nearly told him what I always tell him when he carries on like that: "If you did your work and studied the way you should, you wouldn't have to worry about taking tests." But my wife poked me and gave me this look, and I remembered about the fantasy thing. So I said, "Wouldn't it be great if an announcement suddenly came over the radio—'Snow day today! Major storm expected. All schools closed!'"

That took him by surprise. He actually smiled. So I ramped it up. I said, "Know what would really be great? If *any* day you had a test turned into a snow day."

He gave a kind of half-laugh and said, "Yeah . . . I wish!" But by the time he left for school, he was in a better mood.

Steven

I've been remarried for over a year now, and Amy, my fourteen-year-old, has resented my new wife from day one. Every time I pick up Amy at her mother's house for her weekend with Carol and me, it's the same story. The minute she gets in the car she finds something to criticize about Carol.

And no matter what I say to Amy, I can't seem to get through. I point out how unfair she's being to Carol, how she doesn't give her a chance, how Carol has worked so hard to be her friend. But the more I talk, the more she tries to prove me wrong.

It's a good thing I came to the workshop last week, because the following Sunday, when I picked up Amy, she started right in: "I hate coming to your house. Carol is always hanging around. Why did you have to marry her?"

There was no way I could deal with this and drive, so I pulled over and turned off the ignition. All I could think was, *Take it easy. Don't argue with her. Don't even try to reason with her. Just listen this time. Let her get everything out.* So I said, "Okay, Amy, sounds like you've got a lot of strong feelings there. Is there anything else?"

She said, "You don't want to hear what I have to say. You never do."

"I do now. Because I can hear how angry and unhappy you are."

Well, that did it. Out came a long list of complaints: "She's not as sweet as you think . . . She's a big phony . . . All she cares about is you . . . She just pretends to like me."

I never once took Carol's side or tried to convince Amy she was wrong. I just *oh*-ed and *mmm*-ed and listened.

Finally, she sighed and said, "Oh, what's the use."

I said, "There *is* a use. Because knowing how you feel is important to me."

She looked at me, and I could see she had tears in her eyes. "Know something else?" I said. "We need to make sure we get to spend more time together on weekends—just the two of us."

"How about Carol?" she asked. "Won't she be mad?"

"Carol will understand," I said.

Anyway, later that day Amy and I took the dog for a long walk in the park. Now I can't prove there's any connection, but that weekend was the best Carol, Amy, and I ever had together.

Acknowledge Your Teenager's Feelings

Teen: Oh no! What'll I do? I told the Gordons I'd babysit for them Saturday, and now Lisa called and invited me to her sleepover!

Parent: What you should do is . . .

Instead of dismissing your teen's feelings and giving advice:

Identify thoughts and feelings:
"Sounds as if you're pulled in two directions. You want to go to Lisa's, but you don't want to disappoint the Gordons."

Acknowledge feelings with a word or sound:
"Uhh!"

Give in fantasy what you can't give in reality:
"Wouldn't it be great if you could clone yourself! One of you could babysit and the other could go to the sleepover."

Accept feelings as you redirect behavior:
"I hear how much you'd rather go to Lisa's. The problem is, you gave the Gordons your word. They're counting on you."

Two

We're Still "Making Sure"

I was eager to begin tonight's meeting. At the end of our last session, Jim had taken me aside to express his frustration at not being able to get his teenagers to do what he wanted them to do when he wanted them to do it. I acknowledged the difficulty and told him that if he could hang in there one more week, we'd go into the subject in depth.

As soon as everyone had assembled, I wrote the topic of the evening on the board:

Skills for Engaging Cooperation

"Let's start at the very beginning," I said. "When our kids were little, much of our time with them was spent 'making sure.' We made sure they washed their hands, brushed their teeth, ate their vegetables, went to bed on time, and remembered to say please and thank you.

"There were also things we made sure they didn't do. We made sure they didn't run into the street, climb on the table, throw sand, hit, spit, or bite.

"We expected that by the time they reached their adolescent years, most of the lessons would have been learned. But much to our frustration and exasperation, we find ourselves still on the job 'making sure.' True, our teenagers don't bite or climb on the table anymore, but most still need reminders to do their homework, do their chores, eat sensibly, bathe periodically, get enough sleep, and get up on time. We're also still making sure there are things they don't do. 'Don't wipe your mouth with your sleeve' . . . 'Don't throw your clothes on the floor' . . . 'Don't tie up the phone' . . . 'Don't use that tone of voice with me!'

"Each home is different. Each parent is different. Each teenager is different. What are the things you feel you need to 'make sure' your teenager does or doesn't do in the course of a day? Let's start with the morning."

Without a moment's hesitation, people began calling out:

"I make sure he doesn't fall back to sleep after the alarm goes off."
"Or skip breakfast."
"Or wear the same clothes three days in a row."
"Or hog the bathroom so no one else can get in."
"Or come late to his first class because he missed the bus again."
"Or pick a fight with her sister."
"Or forget to take her keys and lunch money."

"How about the afternoon?" I asked. "What's on your 'make sure' list?"

"Call me at work as soon as you get into the house."
"Walk the dog."
"Start your homework."
"Don't eat junk food."
"Don't have any friends over of the opposite sex when I'm not home."

"Don't forget to practice the piano (violin, saxophone)."
"Don't leave the house without telling me where you're going."
"Don't tease your sister."

"Now it's evening," I said. "Again, what are your do's and don'ts for your teens?" People thought for a moment and then . . .

"Don't hole up in your room. Spend time with the family."
"Don't drum on the table."
"Don't slump in your chair."
"Don't stay on the phone all night. Finish your homework."
"Don't stay online all night. Finish your homework."
"For once, say okay when I ask you to do something."
"For once, answer me when I ask you what's wrong."
"Don't use up all the hot water for your shower."
"Don't forget to put your retainer on your teeth before you go to bed."
"Don't stay up late. You'll be exhausted in the morning."

"I'm exhausted just listening to this," Laura commented. "No wonder I'm so worn out by the end of the day."

"And it never lets up," a woman named Gail added. "I'm always after my boys—pushing, prodding, poking at them to get this done and that done. And it's been worse since my divorce. Sometimes I feel like a drill sergeant."

"I have another take on it," Michael said. "I think you're being a responsible parent. You're on the job, doing what a parent is supposed to be doing."

"So how come," Gail asked ruefully, "my kids don't do what *they're* supposed to be doing?"

"What my daughter thinks she's supposed to be doing," said Laura, "is give her mother a hard time. She'll argue with me over the least little thing. I'll say, 'Please take your dirty dishes out of your room,' and she'll say, 'Quit bugging me. You're always on my case.'"

There were murmurs of recognition from the group.

"So with teenagers," I said, "sometimes even the simplest, most reasonable request can trigger a short argument or a long battle. To get a better understanding of our kids' point of view, let's put ourselves in their shoes. Let's see how we'd react to some of the typical methods that are used to get teenagers to do what we want them to do. Suppose I play your parent. As you listen to me with your 'adolescent ears,' please call out your immediate, uncensored, visceral response."

Here are the different approaches I demonstrated, and here's how "my kids" reacted:

Blaming and accusing: "You did it again! You put oil in the pan, turned the burner on high, and left the room. What is wrong with you? You could've started a fire!"

"Stop yelling at me."
"I wasn't gone that long."
"I had to go to the bathroom."

Name-calling: "How could you forget to lock your brand-new bike? That was just plain stupid. No wonder it was stolen. I can't believe you could be so irresponsible!"

"I am stupid."
"I am irresponsible."
"I never do anything right."

Threats: "If you don't think it's important enough to do your chores, then I don't think it's important enough to give you your allowance."

"Bitch!"
"I hate you."
"I'll be glad when I'm out of this house."

Orders: "I want you to turn off the television and start your homework. Stop stalling. Do it *now*!"

"I don't want to do it now."
"Quit bugging me."
"I'll do my homework when I'm ready."

Lecturing and moralizing: "There's something we need to talk about. It's your burping at the table. It may be a joke to you, but the fact is, it's just bad manners. And whether we like it or not, people judge us by our manners. So if you must burp, at least cover your mouth with your napkin and say, 'Excuse me.' "

"What did you say? I stopped listening."
"I feel like burping."
"That's so shallow. Manners might be important to you, but they don't matter to me."

Warnings: "I'm warning you. If you start hanging out with that crowd, you're headed for big trouble."

"You don't know anything about my friends."
"What's so great about your friends?"
"I don't care what you say. I know what I'm doing."

Martyrdom: "I ask you to do one little thing for me and it's too much for you. I don't understand it. I work so hard to give you everything you need, and this is the thanks I get."

"Okay, so I'm a rotten kid."
"It's your fault I'm this way. You spoiled me."
"I feel so guilty."

Comparisons: "There's a reason your sister gets all the phone calls. Maybe if you made more of an effort to be friendly and outgoing the way she does, you'd be popular too."

"She's a big phony."
"I hate my sister."
"You always liked her more than me."

Sarcasm: "So you plan to go straight from basketball practice to the dance without showering. Well, you ought to smell wonderful! The girls will be lining up just to get near you."

"Ha, ha . . . you think you're soooooo funny."
"You don't smell so good yourself."
"Why don't you talk straight and say what you mean!"

Prophecy: "All you ever do is blame other people for your problems. You never take responsibility. I guarantee you, if you keep this up, your problems will only get worse and you'll have no one to blame but yourself."

"I guess I'm just a loser."
"I'm hopeless."
"I'm doomed."

"Enough! I'm having a guilt attack," Laura called out. "This is so much like the kind of stuff I say to my daughter. But just now, when I listened as a kid, I hated the way it sounded. Everything I heard made me feel so bad about myself."

Jim looked distressed.

"What are you thinking?" I asked him.

"I'm thinking that a lot of what you demonstrated sounds painfully familiar. As I mentioned last week, my father never hesitated to put me down. I try to be different with my own kids, but sometimes I hear his words come flying out of my mouth."

"I know! Sometimes I feel like I'm turning into my mother," Karen said. "And that's something I swore I'd never do."

"Okay, so now we know what *not* to say," Gail called out. "When do we get to what we *can* say?"

"Right now," I answered, holding up the illustrations I had prepared. "But before I distribute these, please keep in mind that none of the communication skills you're about to see work all the time. There are no magic words that apply to every teenager in every situation. That's why it's important to be familiar with a variety of skills. However, as you look through these pages, you'll see that the basic principle underlying all of these examples is respect. It is our respectful attitude and respectful language that makes it possible for our teenagers to hear us and to cooperate."

Instead of Giving Orders . . .

Orders often create resentment and resistance.

Describe the Problem

By describing the problem, we invite our teenagers to become part of the solution.

Instead of Attacking the Teenager . . .

When we're angry, we sometimes lash out at our teenagers with words that attack or demean them. Result? They either withdraw or counterattack.

Describe What You Feel

When we describe what we feel, it's easier for the kids to hear us and to respond helpfully.

Instead of Blaming . . .

When teenagers are accused, they usually become defensive.

Give Information

When they're given information, simply and respectfully, they're more likely to assume responsibility for what needs to be done.

Instead of Threats or Orders . . .

**Many teenagers react to threats with
defiance or sullen compliance.**

Offer a Choice

We have a better chance of gaining their cooperation if we can substitute a choice that meets our needs and theirs.

Instead of a Long Lecture . . .

Teenagers tend to tune out long lectures.

Say It in a Word

A short reminder focuses their attention and is more likely
to engage their cooperation.

Instead of Pointing Out What's Wrong . . .

**Teenagers usually react to criticism by defending
their behavior.**

State Your Values and/or Expectations

When parents state their expectations, clearly and
respectfully, teenagers are more likely to listen and
to try to live up to those expectations.

Instead of Angry Reprimands . . .

**Teenagers can be especially sensitive to
their parents' disapproval.**

Do the Unexpected

By substituting humor for criticism, we change the mood and encourage everyone's playful spirit.

Instead of Nagging . . .

**Some teenagers are slow to respond
to a reasonable reminder.**

Put It in Writing

**Often the written word can accomplish what the
spoken word cannot.**

Comments flew as people leafed through the pages and studied the drawings:

"This isn't just for teenagers. I wouldn't mind if my husband used some of this stuff on me."

"*On* you?"

"Okay, *with* me. *For* me. The point is, it would probably improve a lot of marriages."

"I'll bet there are people who would look at these skills and say, 'There's nothing new here. It's just common sense.'"

"But it isn't common. If it were, we wouldn't all be here tonight."

"I'll never remember all this. I'm taping these cartoons to the inside of my closet door."

A father who was new to the group and who hadn't spoken before raised his hand. "Hi, I'm Tony, and I know I probably should keep my mouth shut because I wasn't here last week. But to me these examples only show how to handle the ordinary, everyday small stuff—a dirty backpack, a ripped shirt, bad table manners. I came here tonight because I thought I was going to find out how to deal with the kind of things teenagers do that worry the hell out of their parents—like smoking, drinking, having sex, taking drugs."

"Those are major worries today," I agreed. "But *it's how we handle the 'ordinary, everyday small stuff' that lays the groundwork for handling the 'big stuff.'* It's how we deal with the dirty backpack or ripped shirt or bad table manners that can either improve a relationship or worsen it. It's how we respond to our children's ups and downs that can cause them to pull away from us or to draw closer. It's how we react to what they've done or haven't done that can either stir up resentment or create trust and strengthen their connection to us. And sometimes it is only that connection that can keep our teenagers safe. When they're tempted, conflicted, or confused, they'll know where to turn for guidance. When the unwholesome voices in the pop culture call to them, they'll have another voice inside their heads—yours—with your values, your love, your faith in them."

After a long silence, Tony asked, "Is our meeting over?"

I checked my watch. "Just about," I told him.

"Good," he said, waving his set of cartoons, "Because I'm going to try some of this out tonight, and I want to get home while the kids are still up."

The Stories

In the following stories, you'll see how the parents used their new skills singly, in combination, and sometimes in situations that went beyond the "everyday, small stuff."

Gail

This last session was made-to-order for me. I'm recently divorced, just started working full-time, and if there's anything I desperately need now it's cooperation. Both my boys are in their teens, but they've never been big on helping out—which I know is my fault because I hate nagging, so I always end up doing things myself.

Anyway, Saturday morning I sat them both down and explained that there was no way I could manage my new job and keep on do-ing everything I did before. I told them I needed them to pitch in and that we all had to pull together now as a family. Then I listed all the chores that had to be done around the house and asked each of them to choose any three they'd be willing to be responsible for. Just three. They could even switch jobs at the end of each week.

Their first reaction was typical. Loud complaints about all

the pressure they were under at school and how they "never had time for anything." But finally each of them signed on for three chores. I posted the list on the refrigerator and told them that it was a huge relief just to think about coming home from work and finding the laundry done, the dishwasher unloaded, and the table cleared and set for dinner.

Well, that isn't exactly what happened. But they have been doing some of the chores, some of the time. And when they don't, I just point to the list and they get going.

Now if I had only known this years ago . . .

Laura

My daughter has a new way of letting me know that I've done something that "displeases" her. She gives me the silent treatment. If I dare to ask what's wrong, she shrugs and looks at the ceiling, which infuriates me.

But after last week's meeting, I was all fired up—determined to try something different. She was sitting at the kitchen table having a snack when I came in. I pulled up a chair and said, "Kelly, I don't like what's been going on between us."

She folded her arms and looked away. I didn't let that stop me. I said, "I do something that makes *you* mad; you stop talking to me, which makes *me* mad; then I end up yelling at you, which makes you even more mad. So, Kelly, what I realize now is that I need you to tell me directly if something is bothering you."

She shrugged and looked away again. This kid wasn't going to make it easy for me. "And if that's too hard," I said, "then at least give me a signal, some kind of sign. I don't care what. Knock on the table, wave a dish towel, put a piece of toilet paper on your head. Anything."

She said, "Oh, Mom, don't be crazy," and left the room.

I thought, *I do sound crazy*, but a few minutes later she came back into the kitchen with this funny look on her face and something white on her hair. I said, "What is that thing on your . . . oh, right . . . toilet paper." We both started to laugh. And for the first time in a long time we actually talked.

Joan

Last night my fifteen-year-old announced that she wanted to get her nose pierced.

I went berserk. I started screaming at her. "Are you out of your mind? God gave you a beautiful nose. Why would you want to put a hole in it? Why would you want to mutilate yourself? That is the stupidest idea I ever heard of!"

She screamed back at me. "All I want is one little ring for my nose! You should see what other kids have. Kim has a stud in her tongue, and Briana has a ring in her eyebrow, and Ashley has one in her belly button!"

"Well, they're stupid too," I said.

"I can't talk to you. You don't understand anything," she yelled and stomped out of the room.

I just stood there and thought, *And I'm the mother who's going to a class on communication. Wonderful!* But I wasn't about to give up. I just needed a better way to get through to her.

So I went on the Internet to see what I could find out about body piercing. Well, it turns out that it's illegal for anyone under eighteen in my county to have their bodies pierced, branded, or tattooed without a written, notarized letter from a parent or guardian. The only exception was for ear piercing. And there was this whole section on all the diseases you could get from unclean instruments or unsanitary conditions—hepatitis, tetanus, infections, boils . . .

Well, when she finally came out of her room, I told her that I was really sorry for the things I had said about her and her friends, but there was information on the Internet I thought she should see. Then I pointed to the screen.

She looked at it and said, "Well, nobody I know ever got sick. Anyway, I'm willing to take a chance."

I said, "The problem is, *I'm* not willing to take a chance. Your health is too important to me."

She said, "Okay, so I'll go to a regular doctor and let him do it. All you'd have to do is give me written permission."

I said, "I can't go along with that. My original objection still stands. Besides, I know myself. Just seeing my daughter walking around with a ring sticking out of her nostril would be extremely upsetting to me. And I don't want to be upset every time I look at you. When you turn eighteen, if it's still important to you, you can decide then whether or not you want to do it."

Well, she wasn't exactly thrilled with my decision, but she seems to have accepted it. At least for now.

Tony

My fourteen-year-old, Paul, walks around the house as if he's off in another world. If I ask him to do something, he'll say, "Yeah sure, Dad," and that's the end of it. In one ear and out the other. So last weekend I "did the unexpected." Twice.

First time: in a loud, Count Dracula voice, I said, "I vont you to take out der garbage." He looked up at me and blinked. "And don't make me vait," I said. "Vaiting makes me *vild*!!!"

He laughed and said, "Vell, den I better do it."

Second time: I noticed a bowl with leftover cereal on the floor of his room. I pointed to it and in my regular voice I said, "Paul, do you know what this is?"

He said, "Yeah, a bowl."

I said, "Nope. It's a party invitation."

"A what?"

"An invitation to all the cockroaches in the neighborhood to come into Paul's room and party."

He grinned. "Okay, Dad, I get the message," and he actually picked up the bowl and brought it into the kitchen.

I know "funny" won't always work. But it's nice when it does.

Michael

My daughter hit me with a zinger this week. She said, "Now, Daddy, I'm going to ask you something and I don't want you to freak out and say no. Just listen."

"I'm listening," I said.

"For my sixteenth birthday party, I want to serve wine. Now, before you get all excited, you have to know that a lot of kids my age have wine at their birthday parties. It's a way of making the night special."

She must have read the disapproval on my face because she stepped up her campaign. "Okay, maybe not wine, but if I can't at least have beer, no one will even want to come. Actually, I wouldn't have to provide it, but if my friends could bring their own, that would be okay. Come on, Daddy. It's no big deal. No one will get drunk. I promise. We just want to have fun."

I almost gave her a flat-out no, but instead I said, "Jenny, I see that this is important to you. I need to think about it."

When I told my wife what Jenny wanted, she went right to her notes from last week and pointed to "put it in writing." She said, "If you write it, she'll read it. If you say it, she'll just argue with you."

Here's the letter I wrote:

Dear Jenny,

Your mother and I have given serious thought to your request that wine be served at your birthday party. For the following reasons, we can't say yes.

1. *In this state it is illegal to serve alcohol to anyone under twenty-one.*

2. *If we were to ignore the law and someone at your party had a car accident on the way home, we, as your parents, would be held legally responsible. Even more important, we'd feel morally responsible.*

3. *If we looked the other way and let your friends bring their own beer, in effect we'd be saying, "It's okay for you kids to break the law as long as we parents pretend we don't know what's going on." That would be dishonest and hypocritical.*

Your sixteenth birthday is a milestone. Let's talk about how we can celebrate the occasion in ways that are safe, legal, and fun for everyone.

Love,
Dad

I slipped the letter under her door. She never mentioned it, but later that day, after some phone calls with her friends, she came to us with a few proposals that "might make up for not having 'real' drinks"—an Elvis impersonator, a karaoke party, or someone who does horoscopes.

It's all still in the discussion stage. But one thing my wife and I know, whatever is decided, we plan to be around that night. We've heard that sometimes kids will leave a party, get a few drinks they've stashed in the car, and come back in—all smiling and innocent. We've also heard of kids bringing their own bottled water to a party, only the "water" is actually vodka or gin. So no, we won't be intrusive. We'll try to be discreet. But we'll be keeping our eyes open.

Linda

Remember I said I was going to tape the cartoons to the inside of my closet door? Well, that's what I did. And it was a big help. Whenever I was about to yell at the kids this week, I'd catch myself, go into my bedroom, open the closet, look over the cartoons, and even though my situation was different, I'd get a better idea of how to handle it.

But last Friday my son was late for school, which meant I was going to be late for work. And I lost it. "You're thirteen years old and still have no sense of time. Why do you always do this to me? I bought you a new watch. Do you ever wear it? No. And don't you dare walk away while I'm talking to you!"

He stopped, threw me a look, and said, "Ma, go read your door!"

To Engage a Teenager's Cooperation

Instead of ordering ("Turn that music down! And I mean *now*!!"), you can:

Describe the problem: "I can't think or have a conversation when the music is blasting."

Describe what you feel: "It hurts my ears."

Give information: "Frequent exposure to loud sound can damage a person's hearing."

Offer a choice: "What would you rather do—turn the volume way down or lower it a little and close your door?"

Say it in a word: "The volume!"

State your values and/or expectations: "We all need to tune in to each other's tolerance for loud music."

Do the unexpected: Put your hands over your ears, make a motion of turning the volume down, place palms together, and bow in a gesture of gratitude.

Put it in writing: Music this loud
May be cool for a crowd
But for just me and you
It is much too, too
LOUD!!!

Three

To Punish or Not to Punish

Our third session hadn't started yet. People were still clustered in small groups, deeply engrossed in conversation. Scraps of sentences reached my ears.

"After what she did, I'm grounding her for the month!"

"So I said to myself, No more Mr. Nice Guy. I've been too easy on this kid. This time he's going to be punished."

Well, I thought to myself, *we haven't talked about punishment yet, but it sounds as if some people are more than ready.*

"Laura, Michael," I said. "Would you be willing to let us all in on what your kids did that made you so angry at them?"

"I wasn't just angry," Laura sputtered. "I was worried sick! Kelly was supposed to be at her friend Jill's birthday party at six o'clock. At seven I got a call from Jill's mother. 'Where's Kelly? She knew we had to be at the bowling alley by seven-thirty. It was on the invitation. Now we're all standing around in our coats waiting for her.'

"My heart began to pound. I said, 'I don't understand. She left in plenty of time. She should have been there long ago.'

" 'Well, I'm sure there's nothing to worry about. I just hope she gets here soon,' Jill's mother said, and hung up.

"I made myself wait fifteen minutes before calling back. Jill answered the phone. 'No, Kelly still isn't here. And I even reminded her in school today not to be late.'

"Now I really started to panic. Horrible pictures flashed through my mind. Twenty agonizing minutes later the phone rang. It was Jill's mother. 'I thought you'd like to know that Kelly has finally arrived. Evidently she met some boy on the way here and was so busy talking to him she forgot we were waiting for her. I only hope we didn't lose our reservation at the bowling alley.'

"I apologized for my daughter and thanked her for calling. But when Kelly walked in after the party, I tore into her: 'Do you realize what you put me through? How could you be so inconsiderate? How could you be so irresponsible? You never give a thought to anyone but yourself. It was Jill's *birthday*. But did you feel an obligation to your friend? No! All you care about is boys and having fun. Well, the fun is over, young lady. You are grounded for the rest of the month! And don't think I am going to change my mind, because I won't.'

"Well, that's what I said to her then. But now I don't know. . . . Maybe I was too hard on her."

"Seems to me," Michael commented, "Kelly got exactly what she deserved. And so did my son."

All heads turned toward him. "What happened?" someone asked. "What did he do?"

"It's what he hasn't been doing," Michael answered. "Namely, his homework. Ever since Jeff made the team, soccer is all he cares about. Every day he comes home late from practice, disappears into his room after dinner, and when I ask him if he's keeping up with his homework, he says, 'Not to worry, Dad. I'm on top of it!'

"Well, Sunday, when Jeff was out, I walked by his room and noticed a letter lying on the floor near his door. I picked it up and saw it was addressed to me. It had been opened and was dated a week ago. Guess what? It was a warning notice from his math teacher. Jeff had handed in no homework—*none*—for the past two weeks. When I saw that, I hit the roof.

"As soon as he walked through the door, I was ready for him. I held up the letter and said, 'You lied to me about doing your homework. You opened mail that was addressed to me. And you never showed me this warning notice. Well, I have news for you, mister. No more soccer for you for the rest of the term. I'm calling the coach tomorrow.'

"He said, 'Dad, you can't do that to me!'

"I said, 'I'm not doing anything to you, Jeff. You've done it to yourself. Case closed.'"

"But is it really closed?" Laura asked.

"Jeff doesn't think so. He's been working on me all week to get me to change my mind. So has my wife." Michael glanced at her meaningfully. "She thinks I'm being too tough. Don't you, dear?"

"What do *you* think?" I asked Michael.

"I think Jeff knows now that I mean business."

"Yeah," Tony chimed in. "Sometimes punishment is the only way to get a kid to shape up—to be more responsible."

"I wonder," I asked the group, "does punishment make a child more responsible? Take a moment and think back to your own experiences when you were growing up."

Karen was the first to respond. "Punishment made me *less* responsible. When I was thirteen, my mother caught me with a cigarette and took away my phone privileges. So I smoked even more. Only I did it in the backyard where no one could see me. Then I'd come in and brush my teeth and say, 'Hi Mom,' with a big smile. I got away with it for years. Unfortunately, I'm still smoking."

"I don't know," Tony said. "To my way of thinking, there's a time and place for punishment. Take me, for instance. I was a bad kid. The gang I hung out with used to get into a lot of trouble. We were a wild bunch. One of the guys ended up in jail. I swear, if my father hadn't punished me for some of the things I did, I don't know where I'd be today."

"And I don't know where *I'd* be today," Joan said, "if I hadn't had therapy to help me undo the effects of all the times I was punished."

Tony looked startled by her comment. "I don't get it," he said to her.

"Both my mother and father," Joan explained, "believed that if a child did anything wrong and you didn't punish her, you weren't a responsible parent. And they always told me they were punishing me for my own good. But it wasn't good for me. I became an angry, depressed teenager who had no confidence in herself. And there was no one I could talk to at home. I felt very alone."

I found myself sighing. What people had just described was all the familiar fallout of punishment. Yes, some children become so discouraged by punishment and feel so powerless that they begin to lose faith in themselves.

And yes, some children, like Tony, conclude that they really are "bad" and need to be punished in order to become "good."

And yes, some, like Karen, become so angry and resentful that they continue their behavior but devise ways not to get caught. They become, not more honest, but more cautious, more secretive, more crafty.

Yet punishment is widely accepted as a preferred method of discipline. In fact, many parents see discipline and punishment as one and the same. How could I share my conviction that *in a caring relationship there is no room for punishment*?

Aloud I said, "If we were somehow forced to eliminate punishment as a disciplinary tool, would we then be completely helpless? Would our teenagers rule the roost? Would they become wild, undisciplined, self-absorbed, spoiled brats, devoid of any sense of right or wrong, who walk all over their parents? Or might there be methods other than punishment that could motivate our teenagers to behave responsibly?"

On the board I wrote:

Alternatives to Punishment

- State your feelings.
- State your expectations.
- Show how to make amends.
- Offer a choice.
- Take action.

I asked Laura and Michael if they'd be willing to try to apply these skills to their current situations with their children. They both agreed to take on the challenge. On the following pages you'll see, in cartoon form, the results of our struggle to work out scenarios that would meet the new guidelines. First we looked at how Laura might deal with her daughter Kelly, whose disregard for time had caused her mother such great concern.

Alternatives to Punishment

State Your Feelings

State Your Expectations

Show How to Make Amends

Offer a Choice

But suppose Kelly repeats her offense? Suppose Mom receives another "Where's Kelly" call? The next time Kelly wants to visit a friend, Mom can

Take Action

The group was impressed. Many comments ensued:

"I was afraid when you first talked about alternatives to punishment that you meant some kind of 'nicey-nice' approach where the parent gives the kid a little scolding and lets her off the hook. But this is strong. You say what you feel and what you expect and give her a way to take responsibility for her behavior."

"And you're not being mean or harsh or making the girl feel like a bad person. You're being tough, but respectful. Respectful to her and respectful to yourself."

"Yeah, it's not you, the parent, who's the enemy. You're on the kid's side, but you're holding her to a higher standard."

"And showing her how to meet it."

"And you're not sending the message 'I have all the power over you. I won't let you do this . . . I'm taking away that.' Instead, you're putting the power back in the teenager's hands. The ball is in Kelly's court. It's up to her to figure out exactly what she can do to give her mother peace of mind—like calling if she's delayed, and calling when she arrives, and making sure to call again before she leaves for home."

Laura groaned and held her hand to her head. "I don't know," she said. "Working it out here with all of you, I almost feel confident. But what happens when I'm faced with the real thing? This approach makes a lot of demands on a parent. It means you have to have a whole different attitude. The truth is, punishing a kid is a lot easier."

"Easier for the moment," I agreed. "But if your goals are to help your daughter to assume responsibility and at the same time to maintain a good relationship with her, then punishing her would be self-defeating.

"But you have a point, Laura. This approach does require a shift in our thinking. Suppose we get more practice. Let's see how the skills could be applied to the problem Michael is having with his son."

Alternatives to Punishment

State Your Feelings

State Your Expectations

Show How to Make Amends

Offer a Choice

What if Jeff does his homework, makes up his assignments, but little by little lets his schoolwork slide again? Dad can then

Take Action

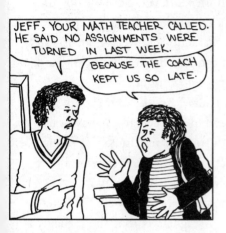

Tony shook his head. "Maybe there's something I'm missing, but I don't see the difference between 'taking action' and punishing Jeff. Either way his father is keeping him off the team."

"Wait, I think I'm finally beginning to get it," Laura said, turning to Tony. "When you punish a kid, you close the door on him. He's got no place to go. It's a done deal. But when you take action, the kid might not like the action, but the door is still open. He still has a chance. He can face up to what he did and try to fix it. He can turn a 'wrong' into a 'right.'"

"I like the way you put that, Laura," I said. "Our goal in taking action is not only to put an end to unacceptable behavior but to give our kids a chance to learn from their mistakes. A chance to right their wrongs. Punishment may stop the behavior, but it may also stop children from becoming self-correcting."

I glanced at Tony. He still looked skeptical. I went on, determined to get through to him. "My guess is that the teenager who has just been grounded for a week does not lie up his room and think, *Oh, lucky me. I have such great parents. They've just taught me a valuable lesson. I'll never do that again!* It's far more likely that the young person will be thinking, *They're mean*, or, *They're unfair*, or, *I hate them*, or, *I'll get back at them*, or, *I'll do it again—only next time I'll make sure I don't get caught.*"

The group was listening intently now. I tried to sum up. "As I see it, the problem with punishment is that it makes it too easy for a teenager to ignore his misdeed and focus instead on how unreasonable his parents are. Worse yet, it deprives him of the work he needs to do to become more mature. More responsible.

"What is it that we hope will take place after a child transgresses? We hope he'll look at what he did that was wrong. That he'll understand why it was wrong. That he'll experience regret for what he did. That he'll figure out how to make sure it doesn't happen again. And that he'll think seriously about how he might make amends. In other words, *for real change to take place, our teenagers need to do their emotional homework. And punishment interferes with that important process.*"

The room was silent. What were people thinking? Did they still have doubts? Had I been clear? Could they accept what they had heard? I looked at my watch. It was late. "We did a lot of hard work here tonight," I said. "I'll see you all next week."

Tony's hand went up. "One last question," he called out.

"Go ahead." I nodded.

"What if you use all the skills we worked on tonight, and the kid still doesn't shape up? Suppose he doesn't know how to be what you call 'self-correcting'? What then?"

"Then that's an indication that the problem needs more work. That it's more complex than it originally appeared and that you need to give it more time and gather more information."

Tony looked bewildered. "How?"

"By problem-solving."

"Problem-solving?"

"It's a process we'll be talking about next week. We'll be working on ways for parents and kids to join forces, explore possibilities, and solve the problem together."

For the first time that evening Tony smiled. "Sounds good to me," he said. "This is one meeting I'm not gonna miss."

The Stories

In the week that followed our session on alternatives to punishment, several people reported how they put their new skills into action.

This first story was told by Tony about his fourteen-year-old son, Paul.

Tony

Paul and his friend Matt came running down the driveway, out of breath, grinning from ear to ear. I said, "What's up, guys?" They said, "Nothing," and looked at each other and laughed. Then Matt whispered something to Paul and took off.

"What did he tell you not to tell me?" I asked Paul. He didn't answer. So I said, "Just tell me the truth. I won't punish you."

Finally, I got it out of him. The story was that he and Matt biked over to the community pool for a swim, but it was closed for the night. So they tried all the doors, found one that wasn't locked, and let themselves in. Then they turned on all the lights and ran around, whooping it up, knocking over all the lounge chairs, throwing cushions everywhere—including into the pool. And to them it was one big joke.

The kid was lucky I promised not to punish him, because believe me, when I heard what he did, I wanted to throw the book at him—cut off his allowance, take away his computer, ground him indefinitely—anything to wipe that stupid smile off his face.

I said, "Listen to me, Paul. This is serious. What you did has a name. It's called vandalism."

His face turned red. He yelled, "See I *knew* I shouldn't have told you. I *knew* you'd make a big deal out of it. It's not like we stole anything or peed in the pool!"

"Well, congratulations for that," I said, "but, Paul, it *is* a big deal. A lot of people in this community worked their tails off to raise enough money to build a pool for their families. They're proud of it, and they work hard to maintain it. And it also happens to be the pool where you learned how to swim."

Paul said, "What are you trying to do? Guilt me?"

"You bet I am," I said, "because what you did was wrong and now you need to make it right."

"What do you want me to do?"

"I want you to go back to the pool—*now*—and put everything back the way you found it."

"Now?! . . . Jeez, I just got home!"

"Yes, now. I'm driving you."

"What about Matt? It was his idea. He should come too! I'm calling him."

Well, he did call, and at first Matt said, "No way," that his mother would kill him if she found out. So I got on the phone. I said, "Matt, the two of you did it, and the two of you need to fix it. I'll pick you up in ten minutes."

Anyway, I drove the kids back to the pool. Luckily, the door was still open. The place was a wreck. I told the boys, "You know what you have to do. I'll wait in the car."

About twenty minutes later, they came out and said, "It's all done. Wanna see?" I said, "Yeah, I do," and went inside to check.

Well, the whole place was straightened up. The lounge chairs were all lined up, and the cushions were back where they belonged. I said, "Good. Everything looks normal. Turn off the lights and let's go."

On the way home the boys were quiet. I don't know about Matt, but I think Paul finally understood why he shouldn't have done what he did. And I think he was glad he had a chance to, as you say, "make amends."

Joan

I was making dinner when Rachel walked through the door. I took one look at her bloodshot eyes and dopey smile, and I knew she was "high." I wasn't sure it was pot, but I was hoping it was nothing worse.

I said, "Rachel, you're stoned."

She said, "You're always imagining things about me," and disappeared into her room.

I just stood there. I couldn't believe it. This was the same child who just last month had confided to me, "Swear you won't tell anybody, Mom, but Louise started smoking pot. Can you believe it? Isn't that terrible?"

I remember thinking *Thank God, it's not my daughter.* And now this! I didn't know what to do. Should I ground her? Forbid her to go anywhere after school? (Certainly not to Louise's!) Insist that she come straight home from now on? No, that would only lead to arguments and tears. Besides, it wasn't realistic.

But I couldn't pretend it didn't happen. And I knew there was no point in trying to talk to her until the effects of whatever she had taken or smoked had worn off. Also, I needed time to think. Should I tell her about my own "experimenting" as a teenager? And if I do, how much should I tell her? Would it help her to know? Or would she use it as an excuse to justify what she was doing ("You did it and you're okay")? Anyway, over the next few hours, I had a dozen imaginary conversations with her. Finally, after dinner, when she seemed more herself, we talked. Here's how the real thing went:

"Rachel, I'm not looking for a confession, but I saw what I saw and I know what I know."

"Oh, Mom, you're so dramatic! It was just a little pot. Don't tell me you never tried it when you were my age."

"Actually, I was a lot older. Sixteen, not thirteen."

"*See* . . . and you're okay."

"I wasn't so okay then. My old friends, what you'd call the 'good kids,' stopped being friends with me, and my grades went way down. The truth is, when I started I had no idea what I was getting myself into. I thought it was harmless. Not as bad for you as cigarettes."

"So what made you stop?"

"Barry Gifford, a boy in my class. He crashed his car into a tree after leaving a party where everyone was getting high. Anyway, Barry ended up in the hospital with a ruptured spleen. Then a few days later we all had to go to this drug awareness program, and they handed out these pamphlets. After that I decided it wasn't worth it."

"Oh, they were probably just trying to scare you."

"That's what I thought. But then I read the whole pamphlet. Some of it I already knew, but there was a whole lot of stuff I didn't know."

"Like what?"

"Like how pot can stay in your system for days after you take it. How it messes up your memory and your coordination, and even your menstrual cycle. And how it's even worse for you than cigarettes. I had no idea that marijuana had more cancer-causing chemicals than tobacco. That was a big surprise to me."

Rachel suddenly looked worried. I put my arm around her and said, "Listen, daughter of mine, if I could, I'd follow you around day and night to make sure that nobody ever gives you or sells you anything that could do you harm. But that would be pretty crazy. So I have to count on you to be smart enough to protect yourself from all the garbage that's out there. And I believe you will. I believe you'll do what's right for your life—no matter how much people pressure you."

She still looked worried. I gave her a big hug and that was that. We didn't talk about it anymore. I think what I said had an impact, but I'm not taking any chances. Kids lie to their parents about drugs (I know—I did), so even though I have mixed feelings about snooping, I think I'll be checking her room every so often.

Gail

Neil, my fifteen-year-old, asked me if Julie, his friend since childhood, could sleep over on Saturday. Her parents were going to an out-of-town wedding, and her grandmother, who had planned to stay with her, got sick and couldn't come.

I thought, *Why not?* My younger son would be spending the weekend at his father's house, so Julie could have his room. Of course I checked with Julie's mother to see how she felt about it. She jumped at the offer—relieved that a responsible adult would be looking after her daughter for the night.

When Julie came, I showed her where she'd be sleeping. Then the three of us had a nice dinner and watched a video.

The next morning Julie's mother called to say she was back home and could she speak to Julie. I went upstairs to get her. The door of her room was half-open, and the bed had not been slept in! The pillows that I had arranged so carefully the day before were exactly as I had left them. As I stood there with my mouth open, I heard laughter coming from Neil's bedroom.

I rapped hard on his door and yelled out that Julie's mother was on the phone and wanted to speak to her.

When the door finally opened, Julie came out looking rumpled and embarrassed. She avoided my eyes, ran downstairs to talk to her mother, ran back upstairs to get her backpack, thanked me "for everything," and went home.

As soon as she left the house, I exploded. "Neil, how could you do this to me!? I gave Julie's mother my word that I would be responsible for her. That she'd be safe and protected!"

Neil said, "But Mom, she . . ."

I cut him off. "Don't 'but Mom' me. What you did was inexcusable."

"But, Mom, nothing happened."

"Oh, *right*. Two teenagers spend the night together in the same bed and nothing happened. You must think I'm pretty stupid. Well, I'll tell you something that won't be happening next weekend. You're not going on the ski trip with your class."

I said it, and I meant it, and I felt it was exactly what he deserved. Then I left the room so I wouldn't have to listen to him carry on about how unreasonable I was being.

A few minutes later I changed my mind. How could keeping Neil from his ski trip help him realize why he shouldn't have done what he did? So I walked back into his room and said, "Listen, Neil, forget what I said about the ski trip. Here's what I really want to say: I know sex is a normal, healthy part of life, but the fact is, parents worry when it comes to their kids. They worry about their daughters becoming pregnant, about their sons becoming fathers. They worry about AIDS and all the other . . ."

He didn't let me finish. He said, "Ma, enough! I don't need a sex education lecture. I know all that stuff. Besides, I'm trying to tell you, *nothing happened*! We were just lying on the bed, watching TV."

Well, maybe they were and maybe they weren't. I decided to give him the benefit of the doubt. I said, "I'm glad to hear it, Neil. Because when you invited Julie to spend the night in our home, you took on a responsibility—to both Julie and her mother . . . and *me*. A responsibility that needed to be honored."

Neil didn't say anything, but from the expression on his face, I could see that my words hit home. And that was enough for me. I was able to drop it.

Jim

My wife and I thought we had covered all bases when we bought
our new computer. We put it in the family room (over the objections of twelve-year-old Nicole, who lobbied hard to have it
in her bedroom); we installed the latest filtering software (we
heard there were at least three million porn sites a kid could accidentally tap into); and we worked out a loose schedule to try to
meet the needs of everyone in the family. We also made it clear
to Nicole that the computer was strictly off-limits after nine P.M.
and was only to be used for schoolwork or to go online with
friends.

Sounds good, doesn't it? Well, a few nights ago I woke up a
little after midnight, saw a light in the family room, got up to
turn it off, and found Nicole glued to the computer. She was so
absorbed, she didn't even hear me. I stood behind her and read
the screen: "Courtney, you sound so cute and funny and sexy.
When can I meet you?" The second she realized I was there, she
typed in "pos" (I later learned that means "parent over shoulder") and blanked out the screen.

I broke out in a cold sweat. I've heard too many news reports
about what happens to young girls who meet teenage boys in
chat rooms. The boy flatters her, tells her how much they have
in common, makes her feel special, and little by little gets her to
the point where she agrees to meet him. Only it turns out he's
not a cute teenage boy but some old guy, a sexual predator who's
out to do who-knows-what to her.

I said, "Nicole, what the hell do you think you're doing? Do
you have any idea what kind of danger you're exposing yourself
to? I ought to take away your computer privileges indefinitely!"

She immediately went on the defensive. She said there was

nothing to get so excited about, that she was only having a little fun, that she hadn't even used her real name, and that she was smart enough to know the difference between a "sicko creep" and a normal person.

I said, "Nicole, listen to me. There is *no way* you can tell the difference! The worst 'sickos' are capable of sounding completely normal and charming. They know exactly how to go about fooling a young girl. They've had lots of practice." Then I told her that I wanted her password because from now on her mother and I would be checking regularly to see where she'd been online.

Her reaction? I didn't trust her . . . I had no right . . . I was taking away her privacy, etc., etc. But by the time I finished telling her some of the horror stories I had heard about how these "normal" guys turn out to be stalkers, kidnappers, rapists, or worse, all she could manage to say, in a weak little voice, was, "Well, you can't believe everything you hear."

I guess she was trying to save face. But I think a part of her was actually relieved that her father was looking out for her and that he wasn't a pushover.

Alternatives to Punishment

Teen: You swore you'd quit smoking, and you're still do-
          ing it! You are such a phony. You are so full of it!
Parent: And *you*, big mouth, are grounded this weekend!

Instead:

State your feelings:
"That kind of talk makes me angry."

State your expectations:
"When I'm trying to stop smoking, what I expect from my son is support—not an attack."

Offer a choice:
"Name-calling hurts. You can either talk to me about what you think might help me quit or you can put it in writing."

Show how to make amends:
"When you realize you've offended someone, it's a good idea to apologize."

But what if the teenager continues to speak disrespectfully?

Take Action (as you leave the room):
"This conversation is over. I'm not available for insults."

Four

Working It Out Together

Karen began the session even before everyone had settled down. "I couldn't wait to get here tonight. Remember last week when Tony asked what if none of the alternatives to punishment work? You said something about problem-solving. Anyway, I've got a big problem going on now with Stacey, and I have no idea how to solve it."

"The good news," I said, "is that you don't have to solve it by yourself. The five-step method you'll be learning today shows how parents and teens can sit down and tackle the problem together."

"Sit down?" Laura exclaimed. "Who has time to sit down? In my house everyone is always rushing off somewhere. We talk to each other on the run."

"People do have hectic schedules these days," I said. "It isn't easy to find the time. Yet time is what this process requires. You can't think together creatively if either one of you is rushed or agitated. For this approach to yield results, it's best to wait until both parties are relatively calm."

"Yeah," Tony said, "but the minute you let a kid know you

want to talk to him about something he's doing that you don't like, no matter how calm *you* are about it, *he's* not going to be so calm anymore."

"And that," I said, "is why your very first step, after bringing up the problem, is to invite your teenager to tell his or her side of the story. That means putting your feelings on hold, temporarily, and listening to her. Once she knows her point of view has been heard and understood, she'll be much more likely to be able to hear what you have to say."

"And then?" Karen asked impatiently.

"And then," I said, "it's a matter of the two of you putting your heads together and trying to figure out something that might work for both of you. Suppose I illustrate by using an example from my own home.

"When my son was about fourteen, he discovered heavy metal. He'd play that music—if you can call it that—so loud the windows rattled. I asked him to please turn it down. Nothing. I yelled at him to turn it down. Still nothing. I tried all of the skills we talked about in our session on engaging cooperation: I described, I gave information, I offered choices, I wrote a note . . . I even used humor. I thought I was very funny. He didn't.

"One night I lost it. I stormed into his room, unplugged his tape player, and threatened to take it away permanently. You can imagine the screaming match that followed.

"I had a hard time falling asleep that night. The next day I decided to try the one approach I hadn't used—problem-solving. I waited until after breakfast before even venturing to bring up the subject. But the minute I mentioned the word 'music,' his back went up. He said, 'Oh no, not that again!' I said, 'Yes, *that* again. Only this time I want to try to see things from your point of view. . . . I'd like to really understand where you're coming from.'

"That took him by surprise. He said, 'It's about time!' Then he let me know exactly how he felt: 'I think you're much too sensitive. The music isn't *that* loud—it has to be loud enough to feel the beat and hear the lyrics. Because the lyrics are great, even though you hate them. But if you ever really listened to them, maybe you'd like them too.'

"I didn't argue with him. I acknowledged everything he said, and then I asked if he could listen to how I felt.

"He said, 'I know how you feel. You think it's too loud.'

" 'You're right. I try not to let it bother me, but it does.'

" 'So wear earplugs.'

"Again I didn't argue. I wrote it down and said, 'That's our first idea! Let's see what else we can think of that might work for both of us.'

"Well, we came up with all kinds of possibilities—everything from his wearing headphones to soundproofing his room to putting a rug on his floor to turning down the volume *a little,* to closing bedroom and kitchen doors.

"When we finally reviewed our list, we quickly eliminated earplugs for me (I didn't want to walk around with my ears plugged up), headphones for him (loud volume could damage his hearing), and soundproofing (too expensive). However we did agree that a rug on his floor, closing doors, and lowering the volume—even a little—would help. But it turned out that what he really wanted was for me to listen to his music with him—to 'at least give it a chance.'

"Well, I did listen, and after a while I could sort of see why the music might appeal to him. I even began to understand why the words that were so distasteful to me might be satisfying to kids. I guess teenagers relate to lyrics that express their anger and frustration.

"Did I grow to love his music? No. But I did become more ac- cepting of it. And I think that because I was willing to spend time with him in his world, he became more willing to accommodate me. Sometimes he'd even ask, 'Mom, is this too loud for you?'

"Well, that was my experience. Now let's see how the same approach might apply to a situation that most of you are probably familiar with—the mess, disorder, chaos, or whatever you call it in a teenager's room."

People laughed knowingly. Michael said, "I call it the 'garbage dump.'"

"In our house," Laura added, "we call it the 'black hole.' Whatever goes in, never comes out."

"And what do you call the kids?"

From around the room I heard, "Slob" . . . "Pig" . . . "You live like an animal" . . . "The way you keep your room, who'd ever want to marry you?"

I reached into my briefcase. "Here's an alternative to that kind of talk," I said and handed out the illustrations that would show the problem-solving process in action—step by step.

On the next few pages you'll see what I distributed to the group.

Working It Out Together

Step I

Invite Your Teen to Give His Point of View

Step II

State Your Point of View

Step III

Invite Your Teenager to Brainstorm with You

Step IV

Write Down All Ideas—Silly or Sensible—
Without Evaluating

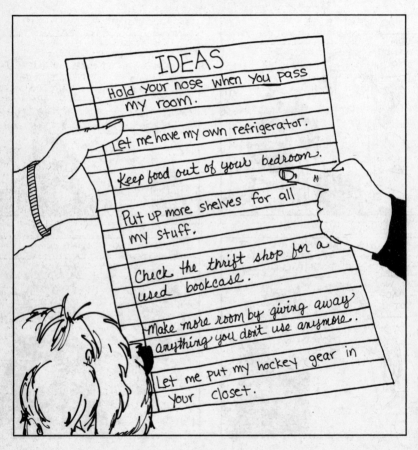

Step V

Review Your List. Decide Which Ideas You Can Both Agree to and How to Put Them into Action.

"I don't mean to be negative," Karen said, "because I can see how this approach could work with a kid whose room is a mess. But that's not a serious problem. Stacey did something this week that really worried me. And I know I got excited and made things worse. But I still don't see how I could have used any of this with her."

"So what did she do?" Laura asked. "Don't keep us in the dark."

Karen took a deep breath. "Okay, here goes. Last Friday my husband and I went out to dinner and a movie. Before we left, Stacey, who's thirteen, asked if two of her girlfriends could come over, and of course we said yes. The movie ended early, and when we got back to the house, we saw two boys running out the side door. My husband ran after them. I went inside.

The minute I opened the door I knew something wasn't right. The windows were wide open, the house was freezing cold, the whole place smelled of cigarette smoke, and Stacey and her girlfriends were in the kitchen stuffing beer cans into the bottom of a garbage bag and covering them with newspapers.

"As soon as she saw me, she said, 'It wasn't my fault.'"

"I said, 'We'll talk later,' and sent the girls home. The minute they were out the door Stacey started telling me this whole long story and giving me all kinds of excuses.

"I told her I wasn't buying any of it and that she knew the rules and deliberately broke them. And then I let her know that her father and I weren't finished with her yet. So that's why I'm here tonight. But problem-solving? I don't know. I really don't see how that could help."

"We won't know unless we try," I said. "Would you be willing to role-play with me?" I asked.

Karen looked uncertain. "What part would I play?"

"Whatever part you want."

She thought a moment. "I guess I should be Stacey. Because I know the kind of thing she'd say. So how do I begin?"

"Since I'm your mom," I said, "and I'm the one who's worried about the problem, it's up to me to start the conversation."

I pulled my chair up to Karen. "I hope this is a good time for you, 'Stacey,' because we need to talk about last night."

Karen (now Stacey) slumped in her chair and rolled her eyes. "I tried to talk to you, but you wouldn't listen!"

"I know," I said, "and that can be frustrating. But I'm ready to listen now." Here's how our dialogue continued:

Stacey:	Like I said, I didn't expect those boys to come. I don't even know them. They're not in any of my classes. They're older.
Mother:	So the boys were a complete surprise to you.
Stacey:	That's right! When I opened the door for Jessie and Sue, these two guys were standing behind them. I never invited them in. I told Jessie my parents would be pissed if I let boys in the house.
Mother:	So you made it very clear that you wanted them to leave.
Stacey:	Yeah, but they said they were just going to stay for a few minutes.
Mother:	And you thought they meant it.
Stacey:	I did. Like, you know, I didn't think they were going to smoke or drink. When I told them not to, they laughed. I didn't even know that Jessie smoked.
Mother:	So you made a real effort to stop them, but no matter what you said, no one would listen. You were in a tough position, Stacey.

Stacey: I really was!

Mother: Stacey, here's how it was for me. It was a shock to come home and see boys running out the door and to smell smoke in the house and find beer cans in the garbage and . . .

Stacey: But, Mom, I just told you, it wasn't my fault!!

Mother: I understand that now. But I want to make sure it doesn't happen again. So to me the big question is, how can you feel comfortable about having your friends over, and how can Dad and I feel confident that our rules are being respected—whether we're home or not?

Stacey: Mom, it's no biggie. All I have to do is tell Sue and Jessie they can't ever bring boys over when you're not home.

Mother: Okay, I'll write that down. It's the first suggestion for our list. Now *I* have a thought: install a peephole in the door. That way you can see who's out there before you open it.

Stacey: And if anyone wants to smoke, I'll tell them they have to go outside.

Mother: We could make some NO SMOKING signs and put them around the house. You could tell everyone your mean mother made you do it. . . . What else?

Suddenly Karen broke out of character. "I know . . . I know we're not finished, and I know we're supposed to go over all the suggestions and decide which ones are best and all that, but I have to tell you what was happening to me when I was playing Stacey. It was so amazing. I felt so respected . . . that my mother really listened to me . . . that it was safe to tell her how I really felt and that she wasn't going to jump down my throat . . . and that I was smart for coming up with some ideas, and that my mother and I were a real team."

I beamed at Karen. In her own inimitable way, she had expressed the core of what I had been hoping to communicate.

I thanked her for throwing herself so fully into her part and for sharing her inner process with us. Several people applauded.

Karen grinned at them. "Don't applaud yet," she said. "The big performance is still ahead. Now the real mother has to go home and pull it off with the real Stacey. Wish me luck, everybody."

From around the room came shouts of, "Good luck, Karen!"

On that high note, the meeting ended.

The Stories

When parents took the time to sit down with their teenagers and try out their new problem-solving skills, they experienced a number of new insights. Here are the highlights of what they reported:

Karen: Problem-solving can help you learn what's really going on.

When I left the session last week, I didn't know whether Stacey would even be willing to talk to me. There was so much bad feeling between us. But as soon as I did the very first step of "the method"—you know, really listening to her point of view and accepting all her feelings—she turned into another person. Suddenly she was telling me things she never would have told me before.

I found out that one of the boys was Jessie's new boyfriend, and that she was laughing and being silly and hanging all over him, and that when he offered her a cigarette she took it and smoked it.

I didn't say a word. I just listened and nodded my head. Then she told me that the boys had a six-pack with them, and when they finished that, they started looking around for something else to drink. One of them found the liquor cabinet, and they both helped themselves to some Scotch. They tried to talk the girls into having "a shot," but only Jessie did.

Boy, did I have to exercise self-control! But I'm glad I did, because the more we talked, the more I understood where Stacey was coming from. I could see that part of her was excited by the whole experience, but mostly I think she was scared and overwhelmed.

Just knowing that made the rest of our discussion a lot easier. I didn't have to spend time explaining how I felt (Stacey already knew my views about smoking and drinking), and it didn't take long for us to come up with a list of solutions. Here's what we both agreed to:

- No boys allowed in the house unless parents are home.
- No alcoholic beverages allowed.
- Anyone who *must* have a cigarette has to go outside.
- Mom will tell Sue and Jessie about the new house rules (in a friendly way).
- Dad will install a lock on the liquor cabinet.
- If adult help is needed and parents can't be reached, call any of the numbers listed on the refrigerator door.

By the time we finished our list, we both felt pretty good. We had worked things out together. Instead of me laying down the law, Stacey had a say in what the law should be.

Laura: It isn't always necessary to go through every step of problem-solving in order to arrive at a solution.

When Kelly came waltzing into my room to model her new outfit for me, she was bubbling over with excitement. "Mom, look what I bought with my birthday money! Isn't it cool? It is so totally in fashion! Don't you love it?"

I took one look at her and thought, *Thank goodness her school has a dress code.* My next thought was, *Okay, maybe this is the time for mother and daughter to do some problem-solving.* I started with the first step—her feelings. "I hear you, Kelly. You love the way that little T-shirt goes with those hip-hugger jeans."

Then I expressed my feelings. "I think that look is too suggestive. I don't want my daughter walking around in public with all that bare skin and her belly button showing. I think it sends the wrong message."

She didn't like hearing that. She plopped down in a chair and said, "Oh, Mom, you are so out of it."

"That may be true," I said, "but can we possibly come up with any kind of solution that would . . ." Before I could even finish my sentence, she said, "So I won't wear it 'in public.' Only in the house, when I'm hanging out with my girlfriends. Okay?"

"Okay," I said. And that ended it. At least temporarily. Because I know the scene today. The girls walk out the door looking like what my mother would call "perfect little ladies." But as soon as they turn the corner, the T-shirts get rolled up, the jeans get yanked down, and once again, the belly button is on display.

Jim: Don't reject any of your teenager's suggestions. Sometimes the worst ideas can lead to the best.

Jared, my fourteen-year-old, has suddenly started complaining that his sister, who's twelve, is driving him crazy. Whenever his friends are in the house, she manages to find reasons to walk into his room and get herself noticed. I understand what's going on, but it makes Jared furious. He yells at her to get out and yells at my wife to keep her out.

One night after dinner I decided to try problem-solving with him. The first step took some self-control. I had to make myself sit there and listen to all his complaints about his sister. And once he got started, he couldn't stop. "She's such a pest . . . She's always hanging around when my friends are over . . . She makes up any excuse to come into my room . . . She needs paper or she wants to show me something . . . And she never knocks . . . And when I tell her to leave, she just stands there like an idiot."

I acknowledged how frustrating that must be for him, but decided to say nothing about how frustrating it was for me to hear him talk that way about his sister. I knew he was in no mood to hear my feelings.

The first thing he said when I told him that we needed some creative ideas to solve this was "send her to Mars."

I wrote it down, and he broke into a big smile. The rest of the list came fast.

- Hang a KEEP OUT sign on my door. (Jared)
- Dad should tell her she *can never* come into my room unless I say so. (Jared)
- Jared should tell his sister himself, calmly and *diplomatically*, that he wants his privacy respected when his friends visit. (Dad)

- Make a deal with her. If she leaves me alone with *my* friends, I won't tease *her* friends when they come over. (Jared)

We left it there. That was a few days ago. Since then, Jared did have a talk with Nicole, and so did I. But the big test is still ahead. His friends will be over for band practice on Saturday.

Michael: When you use the problem-solving approach with your teenagers, they're more likely to try the same approach with you.

I overheard Jeff on the phone telling his friend about this "awesome" rock concert they *had* to go to. When he hung up, he said, "Dad, I really need to talk to you."

I thought, *Uh-oh, here we go again. We're going to have the same old argument: You never let me go anywhere. Nothing terrible is going to happen. Nobody else's father . . . etc., etc.*

But to my amazement, he said, "Dad, Keith wants me to go to a concert this Saturday night. It's in the city. But before you say anything, I want to hear all your objections. All the reasons you wouldn't want me to go. I'll write them down. You know, the way you did with me last week."

Well, I had a long list for him. I told him that I worry about two fifteen-year-old boys standing alone, late at night, at a bus stop. I worry about all the drugs that are passed around at concerts. I worry about muggers and pickpockets looking for easy targets. I worry about injuries from that thing called mosh pits where kids throw themselves off the stage and other kids catch them. Maybe. And I object to the hate lyrics that put down women, police, gays, and minorities.

When I was finished, he looked at his scribbled notes and he actually addressed each of my concerns.

He said he'd make sure that he and Keith stood with other people at the bus stop; that he'd keep his wallet in the inside pocket of his jacket and keep his jacket zipped up; that he and his friends aren't into drugs; that he didn't know if there was going to be a mosh pit, but if there was he'd just watch; and that he's not so weak-minded that some dumb words in a song are going to turn him into a bigot.

I was so impressed by how mature he sounded that I agreed to let him go—under certain conditions: instead of the boys taking the bus, his mother and I would drive them to the city, go to a movie while they were at the concert, and pick them up afterward. "If that plan is okay with you," I said, "then all you'll need to do is call the box office and find out what time the concert lets out."

He thanked me. And I thanked him for taking my concerns seriously. I told him that the way he had approached me helped me to think things through.

Joan: There are some problems that go beyond problem-solving. Sometimes professional help is needed.

At first I thought Rachel had lost weight because of all the exercise she was doing lately. But I couldn't understand why she was tired all the time or why she had no appetite. No matter what I made—even her favorite foods—she'd take one or two bites, push the rest around on her plate, and when I'd urge her to eat more, she'd say, "I'm really not hungry" or "Anyway, I'm too fat."

Then one morning I accidentally walked in on her as she was getting out of the shower and I couldn't believe what I saw. Her body was emaciated. She was skin and bones.

I was completely unnerved. I didn't know if this was the kind of problem we could sit down and solve together, but I had to try. The very first step—acknowledging her feelings—backfired. I said, "Honey, I know I've been on your case lately about how you haven't been eating, and I know that can be irritating, and I can understand why you'd . . ."

Before I could get one more word out of my mouth, she flared up at me: "I don't want to talk about this. It's not your concern. It's *my* body and what I eat is *my* business!" Then she went into her room and slammed the door.

That was when I called our family doctor. I told him what was going on and he urged me to bring Rachel in for a checkup. When she finally came out of her room, I said, "Rachel, I know you don't think your eating should be my concern. But the fact is, I *am* concerned. You're my daughter and I love you and I want to help you, but I don't know how and that's why I made an appointment with the doctor."

Well, she gave me a hard time. ("I don't need help! *You're* the one who has a problem, not me.") But I didn't back down. And when we finally saw the doctor, he confirmed my worst fears. Rachel had an eating disorder. She had lost twelve pounds, missed her last few periods, and her blood pressure was low.

The doctor was very direct with her. He told her she had a potentially serious health problem that required immediate attention, that it was good it was caught early, and that he was referring her to a special program. When she asked, "What kind of program?," he explained that it was a "team" approach—a combination of individual, group, and nutritional counseling.

As we were leaving, Rachel looked overwhelmed. The doctor smiled at her and took her hand. He said, "Rachel, I've known

you since you were a little girl. You're a spunky kid. I've got a lot
of confidence in you. When you go into this program, you're
going to make it work for you."

I don't know if Rachel was able to take in what he said, but I
was grateful for his words and very relieved. I wouldn't have to
face this alone. There was help out there.

Working It Out Together

Parent: This is the second time you missed your curfew! Well, you can forget about going anywhere next Saturday night. You're in for the weekend.

Instead:

Step 1: Invite your teenager to give her point of view.

Parent: Something is making it difficult for you to meet your curfew.

Teen: I'm the only one who has to be home by ten. I always have to leave when everyone is having fun.

Step 2: State your point of view.

Parent: When I expect you home at a certain time and you're still not here, I worry. My imagination goes into overdrive.

Step 3: Invite your teenager to brainstorm with you.

Parent: Let's see if there are any ideas we can come up with that would give you a little more time with your friends and give me peace of mind.

Step 4: Write down all ideas—without evaluating.

1. Let me stay out as long as I want and don't wait up for me. (teen)
2. Never let you out again until you're married. (parent)
3. Move my curfew up to eleven. (teen)
4. Extend your curfew to ten-thirty—temporarily. (parent)

Step 5: Review your list and decide which ideas you want to put into action.

Teen: Ten-thirty is better. But why temporarily?

Parent: We can make it permanent. All you'd have to do is prove you can be on time from now on.

Teen: It's a deal.

Five

Meeting the Kids

I wanted to meet the kids.

I'd been hearing about them, talking about them, thinking about them, and now I wanted to experience them for myself. I asked the parents how they'd feel about my scheduling a few sessions with their children—one to get acquainted, one to teach them some basic communication skills, and then one where we would all meet together.

The response was immediate: "That would be wonderful!" . . . "Great idea!" . . . "I don't know if I can get her to go, but I'll give it my best shot" . . . "Just tell me when. He'll be there."

We set three dates.

————

As I watched the kids pile into the room, I immediately started matching children to parents, trying to figure out who belonged to whom. Was the tall, skinny boy Tony's son Paul? He sort of looked like Tony. Was the girl with the friendly smile Laura's daughter Kelly? But then I thought, *No, don't go there. Get to know these young people as individuals, not as extensions of their mothers or fathers.*

When everyone had settled down, I said, "As your parents have probably told you, I teach methods of communication that can help people of all ages to get along better. But as you well know, 'getting along better' isn't always easy. It means we need to be able to hear each other and, at the very least, make an effort to understand the other person's point of view.

"Now, parents certainly understand their own point of view. But I think what many of them are missing—and that includes me—is a deeper understanding of the younger generation's point of view. That's where all of you come in. I'm hoping today to get a better sense of whatever it is that you believe to be true—either for yourself or for your friends."

The boy who looked like Tony grinned. "So what do you want to know? Just ask me. I'm an expert."

"Yeah, sure," another boy snickered. "On what?"

"We'll soon find out," I said as I handed out the page of questions I had prepared. "Please look these over, see what you're comfortable answering, and then we'll talk."

A hand shot up.

"Yes?"

"Who gets to see what we write?"

"Only me. You don't have to put your name on the paper. No one will know who wrote what. All I care about is your honest feedback."

I wasn't sure they'd want to write after a long school day, but they did. They studied each question, stared out the window, bent over their papers, and wrote quickly and earnestly. When everyone was finished, we went down the list of questions together and discussed each one. Most of the kids read their answers aloud; others added their thoughts spontaneously; and a few listened quietly, preferring to hand in their responses in writing. Here are the highlights of what they had to say:

What do you think people mean when they make a comment like, "Oh well, he's a teenager"?

"That we're immature, that we're all brats and a pain in the neck. But I don't agree. Anyone can act like that, no matter what age they are."

"That all teens are trouble. But that's wrong. It's a put-down. There isn't just one kind of teenager. We're all different."

"They always say, 'You should know better,' or, 'Act your age.' But this is our age."

"It's demeaning and insulting when adults think so little of our capabilities."

"They think they know us. They say, 'We had the same problems when we were young.' But they don't realize that times have changed and problems have changed."

What do you think is the best part of being your age— for either you or your friends?

"Having more privileges. Fewer limits and boundaries."

"Having fun and doing what I like to do."

"Having boyfriends."

"Staying out later on weekends and going to the mall with my friends."

"Enjoying life without the responsibilities I know I'll have later on."

"Getting closer to being able to drive."

"There's the freedom to experiment, but also the security and love of your family to come back to when something goes wrong."

What are some of the things kids your age worry about?

"Not fitting in."

"Not being accepted socially."

"Losing friends."

"Kids worry about what others think about them."

"We worry about the way we look—clothes, hair, shoes, brand names."

"Girls have to be skinny and pretty, and guys have to be cool and athletic."

"We worry about academic competition and having to do a ton of homework every night and passing all our subjects."

"Our future and getting good grades."

"I worry about drugs and violence and terrorists attacking us and stuff like that."

"I worry that there's going to be a school shooting and a lot of people are going to be killed. It's so easy to get a gun."

"Teenagers have a lot of stress. Maybe more stress than their parents. They can say whatever they want to say to us, but no way can we say what we want to say to them."

Is there anything your parents say or do that is helpful to you?

"My parents discuss things with me, and we try to come up with solutions."

"My mom knows when I'm in a bad mood and leaves me alone."

"My mom always tells me I look good—even if I don't."

"My dad helps me if I don't understand my homework."

"Once my dad told me about trouble he got into when he was a kid. That made me feel better when I got into trouble."

"My mother talks to me about things to say if people want me to try drugs."

"My parents always tell me, 'Have an aim or goal in life. As long as you have one, it will keep you on track.'"

Is there anything your parents do or say that's unhelpful?

"They blame things on me that aren't true. Also, when I tell them about something that makes me mad, they say, 'Take a rest,' or, 'Forget about it.' That really pisses me off."

"I hate when they tell me I have a bad attitude. Because no child comes into the world with a bad attitude. That's not how you are inside. Sometimes it's the parents' fault. They can be a bad example."

"My parents criticize my study habits, which is unfair because I do okay in school."

"I hate it when my parents yell at me."

"My parents work too hard. There is never enough time to talk to them. I mean, about everyday stuff."

"Parents shouldn't always criticize and correct their kids. My brother was raised up that way. And now he has trouble with authority. He quit all his jobs because he can't handle authority. I'm like that too. I can't hear correction. I hate correction."

If you could give advice to parents, what would it be?

"Don't say, 'You can tell me anything,' and then freak out and lecture us when we do."

"Don't say things like, 'Are you still on the phone?' or 'Are you eating again?' when you can see that we are."

"Don't tell us not to do something and then do it yourself, like drink or smoke cigarettes."

"If you come home in a bad mood, don't bring your troubles down on us or blame us for your bad day."

"Parents shouldn't act nice on the outside and then at home call you names and hit you and take your respect away. If kids are *mean, it could be because that's what they see at home. So even if parents get frustrated and want to say something mean, they should really try to hold that back."*

"Parents should believe in us. Even if we do something wrong, it doesn't mean we're bad people."

"Don't criticize our friends. You don't really know them."

"Don't make us feel guilty if we'd rather hang out with our friends than be with the family."

"If you want your kids to tell you the truth, then don't ground them for every little thing."

"Even though your kids aren't little anymore, tell them that you love them."

"If there is some way to let your children experience life without being in danger, find that plan and follow it, because that's what we need."

If you could give advice to other teenagers, what would it be?

"Don't do dumb things, like drugs, just to get other kids to like you."

"Be friendly to everyone, even the kids who aren't popular."

"Don't join in when kids pick on someone."

"Don't get other kids in trouble by e-mailing bad stuff about them."

"Develop true, good friendships. Then when life is hard and you have no one else, they'll be there."

"If you want your parents to give you a later curfew, start coming home on time."

"If your boyfriend says he'll dump you if you don't have sex with him, then you should dump him."

"Don't think you can just smoke a few cigarettes once in a while and that's it. Because my friend started out that way, and now she's up to a pack a day."

"If you drink or take drugs, just know that you could be messing up your health and your future. Some kids say, 'I don't care. It's my body and I'll do what I want with it.' But they're wrong. It's not just them who will be hurt. All the people who care about them will be let down and disappointed."

What do you wish could be different about your life—at home, in school, or with friends?

"I wish my parents would realize I'm not a baby anymore and let me do more things, like go to the city with my friends."

"I wish my teachers would ease up on the homework. They all act like theirs is the only subject we take. We have to stay up so late at night to finish everything. No wonder we're tired in class."

"I wish my schedule wasn't so packed with studying and music lessons and that I had more free time to hang out with my friends."

"I wish kids wouldn't act nice to your face and then talk about you behind your back."

"I wish my friends would all get along and not try to make me take sides."

"I wish people didn't judge you by how you look or what you wear. That's why I like to go online. Because then, even if you look weird or ugly, it doesn't matter."

"I wish kids didn't fight over stupid things like, 'I saw you with my guy.' Fights don't solve anything. All that happens is you end up getting suspended, and then your parents punish you too."

"I wish parents wouldn't pressure their kids to be perfect. I mean, we only live this life once, so why can't we just sit back a little and enjoy being a teenager? Why do we have to excel all the time? Yes, we have goals and dreams, but can't we reach them without all this stress?"

When the last question had been answered, everyone looked at me expectantly. I said, "Know what I wish? I wish parents and teenagers everywhere could have heard what you had to say this afternoon. I think they would have gained some important insights that could be very helpful to them."

The kids seemed pleased by my comment. "Before we leave," I asked, "is there anything we haven't talked about that you think parents should be aware of?"

A hand went halfway up, then down, then up again. It was the boy who looked like Tony. "Yeah, you tell them that sometimes we yell and say things that get them all upset. But they shouldn't take it personally. A lot of times we don't even mean it."

"That's right," said the girl whose smile was so much like Laura's. "And tell them not to get crazy when we don't clean our room or do stuff to help out. It's not because we're brats. Sometimes we're too tired or we have things on our mind or we need to talk to our friends."

Another girl chimed in. "And ask the parents how they'd like it if the second they got home from work we'd say to them, 'You left your dirty dishes in the sink again!' or, 'I want you to start making dinner *right now!*' or, 'No TV until you've finished paying all your bills!'"

Everyone laughed.

"Actually," she added, "my mother isn't yelling as much since she's been going to your class. I don't know what she's learning there, but she doesn't go ballistic so much anymore."

"What your mother and all the other parents are learning," I said, "are the same communication skills I look forward to sharing with you next week. We'll be exploring ideas that can help people get along better in all of their relationships."

"All?" one of the girls asked. "Does that mean with our friends too?"

"With your friends too," I assured her. Yet there was something about the way she asked the question that gave me pause.

I hadn't planned to focus on friends in our next session, but suddenly it occurred to me that maybe I ought to. Maybe I should take my cue from the kids. Hearing their many comments today about the importance of their friendships jolted me into a fresh awareness of how much emotion teenagers invest in their interactions with their peers.

"How would you all feel," I asked the group, "about using our next session to see how these communication skills might apply to your relationships with your friends?"

No one answered immediately. The kids looked at one another and then back at me. Finally, someone said, "That's cool." Heads nodded in agreement.

"Then that's what we'll do," I said. "See you next week."

Six

About Feelings, Friends, and Family

"Move your ass, retard!"

"Shut your face, trailer trash!"

The words hit me as I made my way past groups of teenagers milling around their lockers at the end of the school day. The guidance counselor ran down the hall toward me. "I'm so glad I caught you!" she exclaimed. "You're meeting in 307 today. Don't worry, I contacted all the kids and told them about the change."

I thanked her and hurried up the stairs, trying to avoid the stampede of pushing, shoving kids who were racing down.

"Ouch, watch where you're going, dirtbag."

"Watch yourself, loser."

"Hey, butthead, wait for me!"

What was going on? Was this the way teenagers talked to one another today?

By the time I got to room 307, most of the kids were already there waiting outside the door. I waved them in and, as they were settling down, described what I had just heard. "Tell me," I inquired, "is this kind of talk typical?"

They laughed at my naïveté.

"Doesn't it bother you?" I asked.

"Nah, it's just joking around. Everybody does it."

"Not everybody."

"But a lot of kids do."

That stymied me. "As you know," I said, "my work is about relationships. About how the words we use to communicate affect the way we feel about each other. So I need to ask you, seriously, are you telling me you really don't mind getting up and going to school each day knowing that there's a good chance that before the day is over, someone will call you a 'loser' or a 'dirtbag' or something worse?"

One of the boys shrugged. "It doesn't bother me."

"Me either," someone added.

I couldn't let it go. "So no one here objects to this kind of talk?"

There was a short pause.

"I do sometimes," a girl admitted. "And I know I shouldn't because my friends and I, we always call each other names, and it's like we're just kidding around. You know, having fun. But if you fail a test and someone calls you a 'retard'—that happened to me once—or like the time I got a bad haircut and my friend said I looked like a weirdo, then it wasn't so funny. I made believe it didn't bother me. But that was on the outside."

"What do you think would happen," I asked her, "if you didn't make believe, if instead you told your friends how you felt on the inside?"

She shook her head. "That wouldn't be good."

"Because? . . ."

"Because they'd put you down or make fun of you."

"Yeah," another girl agreed. "They'd think that you were too sensitive and that you were trying to be different or better, and then they wouldn't want to be your friends anymore."

Many hands flew up. People had a lot to say:

"But those aren't real friends. I mean, if you have to be phony and pretend you don't care, just to fit in, that sucks."

"Yeah, but a lot of kids will do anything to be accepted."

"That's right. I know someone who started drinking and doing other stuff only because his friends did."

"But that's so dumb, because you should be able to do what you think is right and let your friends do whatever they want to do. I say, 'Live and let live!' "

"Yeah, but that's not the way it works in real life. Your friends have a lot of influence over you. And if you don't go along, you could be cut out."

"So what? Who wants friends like that? I think a real friend is someone you can be yourself with, someone who doesn't try to change you."

"Someone who listens to you and cares about how you feel."

"Yeah, someone you can talk to if you have a problem."

I was touched by what the kids were saying. Their friends were so important to them that some of them were willing to give up a part of themselves in order to be part of the group. And yet they all knew, on some level, what gave meaning to a mutually satisfying friendship.

"We must be on the same wavelength," I said. "Ever since our last meeting, I've been doing a lot of thinking about how the skills I teach to adults might work in teenage relationships. You made it very clear just now that the quality you most value in a friend is the ability to hear, accept, and respect what you have to say. Now, how can that idea be put into practice?"

I reached into my briefcase and pulled out the material I had prepared. "You'll see several examples here of one friend trying to get through to another. You'll also see the contrast between the kind of response that can undermine a relationship and the kind that gives comfort and support.

"Let's go over these pages together," I said as I distributed them to the group. "Would any of you be willing to act out the different parts?"

There wasn't a moment of hesitation. They all wanted to "act it out." Amid bursts of laughter, they read their parts with energy and dramatic flare. As I sat there, looking at the illustrations and listening to the voices of real kids, I felt as if I were watching an animated cartoon.

Instead of Put-downs . . .

**When people are upset, questions and criticism
can make them feel worse.**

Listen with a Nod, a Sound, or a Word

Sometimes a sympathetic sound, grunt, or word can help a friend feel better and think better.

Instead of Dismissing
Thoughts and Feelings . . .

**When a friend brushes your feelings aside, you're not likely
to want to continue the conversation.**

Put Thoughts and Feelings into Words

It's much easier to talk to someone who accepts your feelings and gives you a chance to come to your own conclusions.

Instead of Dismissing Wishes . . .

When a friend dismisses your wishes and puts you down
for even having them, you can feel demeaned and
frustrated.

Give in Fantasy What You Can't Give in Reality

It's easier to deal with reality if a friend can give us what we want in fantasy.

"So what do you think of these examples?" I asked. The kids' responses came slowly.

"It's not the way we talk, but maybe it would be good if we did."

"Yeah, because the example showing the 'wrong' way really makes you feel like junk."

"But you can't just say the 'right' words. You have to mean them or people will think you're being phony."

"In a way a lot of it doesn't sound natural. It's a different way of talking. But maybe if you get used to it . . ."

"I could get used to hearing it. I don't know if I could get used to saying it, and I don't know what my friends would think if I did."

"I think the whole thing is awesome. I wish everybody would talk to everybody this way."

"Would that include kids talking 'this way' to their parents?" I asked.

That stopped them. "Like when?" someone questioned.

"Like when your mother or father is upset about anything."

I could see by their puzzled expressions that this was a new direction for them.

"Just imagine," I went on, "that one night your mother or father comes home from work tired and full of complaints about the day: the traffic was heavy, the computer was down, the boss didn't stop yelling, and everybody had to stay late to make up for lost time.

"Well, you could react by saying, 'You think *you* had a bad day? Mine was a lot worse.' Or you could show you understand with a sympathetic 'Oh,' or by putting your parent's thoughts and feelings into words, or by giving them in fantasy what you can't give in reality."

The group was intrigued by my challenge. There was a short

pause, and then, one by one, they reached out to their imaginary parents:

"Boy, Mom, sounds like you had a hard day."

"It's a real pain when the computer goes down."

"You must hate it when the boss yells."

"It's no fun being stuck in traffic."

"I bet you wish you had a job where you could walk to work."

"And that you never had to stay late again!"

"And that your old boss would retire and you'd get a new one who doesn't yell."

They were all grinning at me now, obviously pleased with themselves.

"Know what?" a girl said. "I'm going to try this tonight with my mother. She's always complaining about her job."

"I want to try it with my dad," a boy said. "A lot of times he comes home late and talks about how tired he is."

"I suspect," I said, "that there are going to be some very appreciative parents out there tonight. And don't forget to bring them to our final meeting next week. It will be interesting to see what happens when we all put our heads together."

Feelings Need to Be Acknowledged

Girl: Briana is such a snob! She walked right by me when she saw me in the hall. She only says hello to the cool kids.

Friend: Don't let it get to you. Why should you care about her?

Instead of denying feelings:

Acknowledge feelings with a sound or word:
"Ucch!"

Identify feelings:
"Even though you know what a snob she is, it can still make you mad. Nobody likes being ignored."

Give in fantasy what you can't give in reality:
"Don't you wish one of the popular kids would give Briana a taste of her own medicine? Walk past her as if she doesn't exist. Then smile and give a big hello to somebody else."

Seven

Parents and Teens Together

Tonight was a first for all of us. As each family entered the room and took their seats, there was an undercurrent of tension. No one knew what to expect. Least of all me. Would the parents be inhibited by the presence of their teenagers? Would the kids hold back knowing their parents were watching them? Could I help both generations feel comfortable with each other?

After welcoming everyone, I said, "We're here tonight to explore ways of talking and listening that can be helpful to all members of the family. Now, that doesn't sound as if it should be hard, but sometimes it is. Mostly because of the simple fact that no two people in any family are the same. We're unique individuals. We have different interests, different temperaments, different tastes, and different needs that often collide and conflict with one another. Spend enough time in any home and you'll hear exchanges like:

'It's so hot in here. I'm opening the window.'
'No! Don't! I'm freezing!'

'Turn that music down. It's too loud!'
'Loud? I can hardly hear it.'

'Hurry up! We're late!'
'Relax. We've got plenty of time.'

"And during the teen years, new differences can develop. Parents want to keep their children safe, protected from all the dangers in the outside world. But teens are curious. They want a chance to explore the outside world.

"Most parents want their teenagers to go along with *their* ideas about what's right or wrong. Some teenagers question those ideas and want to go along with what their friends think is right or wrong.

"And if that isn't enough to fuel family tensions, we also have to deal with the fact that parents these days are busier than ever and under more pressure than ever."

"You can say that again!" Tony called out.

The teenager sitting next to Tony muttered, "And kids these days are busier than ever and under more pressure than ever."

There was a chorus of "yeahs" from the other teenagers.

I laughed. "So it's no mystery," I continued, "why people in the same family, who love one another, could also irritate, annoy, and occasionally infuriate one another. Now then, what can we do with these negative feelings? Sometimes they come bursting out of us. I've heard myself say to my own kids, 'Why do you always do that?' . . . 'You'll never learn!' . . . 'What is wrong with you?' And I've heard my kids say to me, 'That's stupid!' . . . 'You're so unfair!' . . . 'Everyone else's mother lets them' . . ."

There were smiles of recognition from both generations.

"Somehow," I went on, "even as these words are coming out of our mouths, we all know, on some level, that this kind of talk only makes people more angry, more defensive, less able to even consider one another's point of view."

"Which is why," Joan sighed, "we sometimes sit on our feelings and say nothing—just to keep the peace."

"And sometimes," I acknowledged, "deciding to 'say nothing' is not a bad idea. At the very least, we don't make matters worse. But fortunately, silence is not our only option. If ever we find ourselves becoming annoyed or angry with anyone in the family, we need to stop, take a breath, and ask ourselves one crucial question: *How can I express my honest feelings in a way that will make it possible for the other person to hear me and even consider what I have to say?*

"I know what I'm proposing isn't easy. It means we need to make a conscious decision not to tell anyone what's wrong with him or her, but to talk only about yourself—what you feel, what you want, what you don't like, or what you would like."

I paused here for a moment. The parents had heard me expound on this topic many times before. The kids were hearing it for the first time. A few of them looked at me quizzically.

"I'm going to hand out some simple illustrations," I said, "which will show you what I mean. To me, they demonstrate the power that both parents and teenagers have to either escalate or deescalate angry feelings. Take a few minutes to look at these examples and tell me what you think."

Here are the drawings I distributed to the group.

Sometimes Kids Make Parents Angry

When parents are frustrated, they sometimes lash out with angry accusations.

Instead of Accusing . . . Say What You Feel and/or Say What You'd Like

Teenagers are more likely to hear you when you tell them how you feel, rather than how rude or wrong they are.

Sometimes Parents Make Kids Angry

When teenagers are insulted, they're sometimes tempted to
return the insult.

Instead of Counterattacking . . . Say What You Feel and/or Say What You'd Like

Parents are more likely to listen when you tell them what you feel, rather than what's wrong with them.

I watched as people studied the pages. After a few minutes I asked, "What do you think?"

Tony's son Paul was the first to respond. (Yes, the tall, skinny boy was Tony's son.) "I guess it's okay," he said, "but when I get mad, I don't think about what I should or shouldn't say. I just shoot my mouth off."

"Yeah," Tony agreed. "He's like me. Quick on the trigger."

"I understand," I said. "It's very hard to think or speak rationally when you're feeling angry. There have been times my own teenagers have done things that have made me so furious, I've yelled, 'Right now, I'm so mad, I'm not responsible for what I might say or do! You'd better stay far away from me!' I figured that gave them some protection and gave me a little time to simmer down."

"Then what?" Tony asked.

"Then I'd go for a run around the block or take out the vacuum and do all the floors—anything physical, anything that would keep me moving. What helps you cool off when you're really, really angry?"

There were a few sheepish grins. The kids were the first to respond:

"I shut my door and blast my music."

"I say curses under my breath."

"I go for a long bike ride."

"I bang on my drums."

"I do push-ups till I drop."

"I pick a fight with my brother."

I gestured toward the parents. "And you?"

"I go right to the freezer and finish off a pint of ice cream."

"I cry."

"I yell at everyone."

"I call my husband at work and tell him what happened."
"I take a couple of aspirin."
"I write a long, mean letter, and then I tear it up."

"Now imagine," I said, "that you've already done whatever it is you do to take the edge off your anger and that you're a little more able to express yourself helpfully. Can you do it? Can you tell the other person what you want, or feel, or need, instead of blaming or accusing them? Of course you can. But it does take some thought, and it does help to get some practice."

"In the cartoons I just handed you, I used examples from my own home. Now I'd like to ask all of you to try to recall something that goes on in your home that bothers, irritates, or upsets you. As soon as you think of it, please jot it down."

The group seemed startled by my request. "It can be a big thing or a little thing," I added. "Either something that has happened or even something that you imagine could happen."

Parents and kids glanced at each other self-consciously. Someone giggled, and after a few moments everyone started writing.

"Now that you've zeroed in on the problem," I said, "let's try two different ways of dealing with it. First write down what you could say that you suspect would only make matters worse." I paused here to give everyone time to write. "And now what you could say that might make it possible for the other person to hear you and consider your point of view."

The room fell silent as people grappled with the challenge I had set for them. When everyone seemed ready, I said, "Now, will each of you please take your papers and find a parent or a child who is *not* your own and sit next to him or her."

After a few minutes of general confusion—amid sounds of shifting chairs and shouts of, "I still need a kid!" and, "Who wants to be my parent?"—people finally settled down with their new partners.

"Now," I said, "we're ready for the next step. Please take turns reading your contrasting statements to each other and notice your reactions. Then we'll talk about it."

People were tentative about getting started. There was much discussion about who would begin the scene. But once the decision had been made, both parents and teenagers assumed their new roles with conviction. They spoke softly to each other at first and little by little became more animated and louder. A mock fight between Michael and Paul (Tony's son) drew all eyes in their direction.

"But you always put it off till the last minute!"

"I do not! I told you I'll do it later."

"When?"

"After dinner."

"That's too late."

"No, it isn't."

"Yes, it is!"

"Just quit hassling me and leave me alone!!"

Suddenly they both stopped, aware that the room was silent and everyone was looking at them.

"I'm trying to get my kid to start his homework earlier," Michael explained, "but he's giving me a hard time."

"That's because he won't get off my back," Paul said. "He doesn't realize that the more he bugs me to do it, the more I put it off."

"Okay, I give up," Michael said, "now let me try the other way." He took a deep breath and said, "Son, I've been thinking . . . I've been pushing you to start your homework early because that's what feels right to me. But from now on, I'm going to trust you to get started when the time seems right to you. All

I ask is that it get done sometime before nine-thirty or ten at the latest, so that you can get a decent night's sleep."

Paul flashed a big grin. "Hey, 'Pop,' that was much better! I like that."

"So I did okay," Michael said proudly.

"Yeah," Paul replied. "And you'll see, I'll do okay too. I'll do my homework. You won't have to remind me."

The group seemed galvanized by the demonstration they had just witnessed. Several teams of parents and kids volunteered to read their contrasting statements aloud. We all leaned forward and listened intently.

Parent *(accusing):*
"Why do you always have to give me an argument when I ask you to do anything? You never offer to help. All I ever hear from you is, 'Why me? Why not him? I'm busy.'"

Parent *(describing feelings):*
"I hate getting into an argument when I ask for help. It would make me so happy to hear, 'Say no more, Mom. I'm on the job!'"

Teen *(accusing):*
"Why didn't you give me my messages? Jessica and Amy both said they called, and you never told me. Now I missed the game and it's all your fault!"

Teen *(describing feelings):*
"Mom, it's really important to me to get all my messages. I missed out on the game because they changed the day and I didn't find out until it was too late."

Parent *(accusing):*
*"All I ever hear from you is 'Give me . . . ,' 'Get me . . . ,'
'Take me here,' 'Take me there.' No matter what I do for you,
it's never enough. And do I ever get a thank-you? No!"*

Parent *(describing feelings):*
*"I'm happy to help whenever I can. But when I do, I'd like to
hear a word of appreciation."*

Teen *(accusing):*
*"Why can't you be like the other mothers? All my friends can
go to the mall by themselves. You treat me like a baby."*

Teen *(describing feelings):*
*"I hate being home on Saturday night when my friends are all
having fun at the mall. I feel I'm old enough now to take care
of myself."*

Laura, who had been listening with special interest as her
own daughter read the last statement, suddenly let out a
shriek. "Oh no, Kelly Ann! I don't care what you say or how
you say it, I am not letting a thirteen-year-old go to the mall
at night. I'd have to be crazy—with what's going on in the
world today."

Kelly turned red. "Mom, *please*," she entreated.

It took us all a moment to figure out that what had been a
practice exercise for the group was a very real and current conflict between Laura and her daughter.

"Am I wrong?" Laura asked me. "Even if she's with friends,
they're still kids. It's just plain irresponsible to let young girls go
wandering around the mall at night."

"Ma, nobody wanders," Kelly retorted heatedly. "We go into

stores. Besides, it's perfectly safe. There are tons of people around all the time."

"Well," I said, "we have two very different viewpoints here. Laura, you're convinced that the mall is no place for an unsupervised thirteen-year-old at night. You foresee too many potential dangers.

"Kelly, to you the mall seems 'perfectly safe,' and you feel that you should be allowed to go there with your friends." I turned to the group. "Are we deadlocked here, or can we think of anything that would satisfy the needs of both Kelly and her mother?"

The group didn't waste a minute. Both parents and teenagers waded in to solve the problem.

Parent (to Laura): I'll tell you what I do with my daughter. I drive her and her friends there and tell them they can stay two hours. But she has to call me after one hour and call again when she's ready to be picked up. I know it's a pain in the neck for her, but it gives me peace of mind.

Teenage girl (to Laura): You can get Kelly a cell phone. That way, she could call you if she has a problem or you could reach her anytime.

Another parent (to Laura): How about you taking the girls and dropping them off? Hang out with them a little while. Then you do a little shopping for yourself and set a time and place to meet them and bring them home.

Teenage boy (sixteen, tall, and handsome, speaking to Kelly): If you want to go to the mall with your friends, why don't you let your mom come with you?

Kelly: Are you kidding?! My friends would freak out.

Laura: Why? All your friends like me.

Kelly: No way. That would be too embarrassing.

Same handsome teen (smiling at Kelly): Suppose you tell
          your friends to put up with it, just once or twice,
          so your mom can see the scene—where you go,
          what you do. That way, maybe she'll relax.

Kelly (charmed by him): I guess. (*looks questioningly at
          her mother*)

Laura: I would do that.

I was impressed by what I had just witnessed. Even more
striking to me than the swift resolution of the conflict was the
way the group had responded to the standoff between Laura
and Kelly. No one took sides. Everyone showed great respect for
the strong feelings of both mother and daughter.

"You've all just given a clear demonstration," I said, "of a
very civilized way of dealing with our differences. It seems we
have to override our natural tendency to prove ourselves right
and the other person wrong: 'You're wrong about this! And
you're wrong about that!' Why do you suppose it isn't just as
natural for us to point out what's right? Why aren't we just as
quick to praise as we are to criticize?"

There was a short pause and then a flurry of responses. First
from the parents:

"It's a lot easier to find fault. That doesn't take any effort.
But to say something nice takes a little thought."

"That's true. Like last night my son turned his music way
down when he noticed I was on the phone. I appreciated his doing that, but I never bothered to thank him for being so consid-
erate."

"I don't know why kids have to be praised for doing what
they're supposed to do. Nobody praises me for getting dinner on
the table every night."

"My father thought praise was bad for kids. He never complimented me because he didn't want me to get a 'swelled head.'"

"My mother went to the other extreme. She never stopped telling me how great I was: 'You're so pretty, so smart, so talented.' I didn't get a swelled head, because I didn't believe her."

Teenagers joined the discussion:

"Yeah, but even if a kid did believe her parents and thought she was so special, when she goes to school and sees what other kids are like, she could be in for a big letdown."

"I think parents and teachers, they say stuff like, 'Terrific,' or 'Great job,' because they think they're supposed to. You know, to encourage you. But me and my friends, we think it sounds phony."

"And sometimes grown-ups praise you to get you to do what they want you to do. You should've heard my grandmother the time I got this really short haircut. 'Jeremy, I hardly recognized you. You look so handsome! You should keep your hair that way all the time. You look like a movie star!' Yeah, right."

"I don't think there's anything wrong with a compliment if it's sincere. I know I feel great when I get one."

"Me too! I like it when my parents say something nice about me to my face. Actually, I think most kids can use a little praise—now and then."

"I have news for you kids," Tony said. "Most *parents* can use a little praise—now and then."

There was a burst of applause from the parents.

"Well," I said, "you've certainly expressed a wide range of feelings about praise. Some of you like it and wouldn't mind hearing a lot more of it. And yet for some of you it's uncomfortable. You experience praise as either insincere or manipulative.

"Could the difference in your responses have something to do with *how* you're being praised? I believe it does. Words like,

'You're the greatest . . . the best . . . so honest . . . smart . . . generous . . . ' can make us uneasy. Suddenly we remember the times we weren't so great or honest or smart or generous.

"What can we do instead? We can describe. We can describe what we see or what we feel. We can describe a person's effort, or we can describe his achievement. The more specific we can be, the better.

"Can you hear the difference between 'You're so smart!' and 'You've been working on that algebra problem for a long time, but you didn't stop or give up until you got the answer'?"

"Yeah, sure," Paul called out. "The second thing you said is definitely better."

"What makes it better?" I asked.

"Because if you tell me I'm so smart, I think, *I wish*, or, *She's trying to butter me up*. But the second way, I think, *Hey, I guess I am smart! I know how to hang in there until I get the answer*."

"That does seem to be the way it works," I said. "When someone describes what we've done or are trying to do, we usually gain a deeper appreciation of ourselves.

"In the cartoons I'm handing out now, you'll see examples of parents and teenagers being praised—first with evaluation, then with description. Please notice the difference in what people say to themselves in response to each approach."

When Praising Kids

Instead of Evaluating . . .

Describe What You Feel

Different kinds of praise can lead kids to very different conclusions about themselves.

When Praising Kids

Instead of Evaluating . . .

Describe What You See

Evaluations can make kids uneasy. But an appreciative description of their efforts or accomplishments is always welcome.

When Praising Parents

Instead of Evaluating . . .

Describe What You Feel

People tend to push away praise that evaluates them. An honest, enthusiastic description is easier to accept.

When Praising Parents

Instead of Evaluating . . .

Describe What You See

Words that describe often lead people to a greater
appreciation of their strengths.

I noticed Michael nodding his head as he looked over the illustrations.

"What are you thinking, Michael?" I asked.

"I'm thinking that before tonight I would've said that any
kind of praise was better than none. I'm a big believer in people
giving each other a pat on the back. But I'm beginning to see
there are different ways to go about it."

"And better ways!" Karen announced, holding up her cartoons. "Now I understand why my kids get so irritated when I
tell them they're 'terrific' or 'fantastic.' It drives them crazy.
Okay, so now I've got to remember—*describe, describe*!!"

"Yeah," Paul called out from the back of the room. "Cut out
the gushy stuff and say what you like about the person."

I seized upon Paul's comment. "Suppose we all do exactly
that—right now," I said. "Please return to your real family.
Then take a moment to think about one specific thing that you
like about your parent or teenager. As soon as it comes to mind,
put it in writing. What could you actually say to let the other
person know what it is that you admire or appreciate?"

There was a wave of nervous laughter. Parents and kids
looked at each other, looked away, and then down at their papers. When everyone had finished writing, I asked them to ex-
change papers.

I watched quietly as smiles grew, eyes filled, and people
hugged. It was sweet to see. I overheard, "I didn't think you noticed" . . . "Thank you. That makes me really happy" . . . "I'm
glad that helped" . . . "I love you too."

The custodian poked his head in the door. "Soon," I
mouthed to him. To the group I said, "Dear people, we have
come to the end of our final session. Tonight we looked at how
we can express our irritation to each other in ways that are helpful rather than hurtful. And we also looked at ways to express

our appreciation so that each person in the family can feel visible and valued.

"Speaking of appreciation, I want you to know what an enormous pleasure it's been for me to work with all of you over these many weeks. Your comments, your insights, your suggestions, your willingness to explore new ideas and take a chance with them have made this a very gratifying experience for me."

Everyone applauded. I thought people would leave after that. They didn't. They hung around, talked to one another, and then each family lined up to say good-bye to me personally. They wanted me to know that the evening had been important to them. Meaningful. The kids as well as the parents shook my hand and thanked me.

When everyone had gone, I stood lost in thought. Almost everything in the media these days gives a picture of parents and teenagers as adversaries. Yet here tonight I had witnessed a very different dynamic. Parents and teens in partnership. Both generations learning and using skills. Both generations welcoming the opportunity to talk together. Happy to connect with each other.

The door opened. "Oh, we're so glad you didn't leave yet!" It was Laura and Karen. "Do you think we could have one more meeting next Wednesday—just for parents?"

I hesitated. I hadn't planned to go on.

"Because we were all talking in the parking lot about the stuff going on with our kids that we didn't think we should bring up tonight with them sitting there."

"And you wouldn't have to worry about contacting people. We'd take care of that."

"We know it's last-minute, and some people said they couldn't make it, but it's *really* important."

"So would that be okay with you? We know how busy you are, but if you have the time . . ."

I looked into their anxious faces and mentally rearranged my schedule.

"I'll make the time," I said.

Expressing Your Irritation

To Your Teenager

Instead of accusing or name-calling:
   "Who's the birdbrain who left the house and forgot to lock the door?!!"

Say what you feel: "It upsets me to think that anyone could have walked into our home while we were away."

Say what you'd like and/or expect: "I expect the last person who leaves the house to make sure the door is locked."

To Your Parent

Instead of blaming or accusing:
   "Why do you always yell at me in front of my friends? No one else has parents who do that!"

Say what you feel: "I don't like being yelled at in front of my friends. It's embarrassing."

Say what you'd like and/or expect: "If I'm doing something that bothers you, just say, 'I need to talk to you for a second,' and tell me privately."

Expressing Appreciation

TO YOUR TEENAGER

Instead of evaluating her:
"You're always so responsible!"

Describe what she did: "Even though you were under a lot of pressure at your rehearsal, you made it your business to call when you knew you were going to be late."

Describe what you feel: "That phone call saved me a lot of worry. Thank you!"

TO YOUR PARENT

Instead of evaluating him:
"Good job, Dad."

Describe what he did: "Boy, you spent half your Saturday setting up that basketball hoop for me."

Describe what you feel: "I really appreciate that."

Eight

Dealing with Sex and Drugs

The group was smaller tonight. Small enough for us to move to the library and sit comfortably around a conference table. Several people started talking about last week's meeting. How much they had enjoyed it. How much better things were going at home. How, since then, both they and the kids would catch themselves repeating some of the same old negative stuff, smile self-consciously, say, "Do-over!" and start again. And even though the new words sounded a little awkward or unfamiliar, they still felt good.

Karen tried to listen patiently, but I could see that she could barely contain herself. At the first break in the conversation, she blurted out, "I'm sorry to be negative, and I'm even sorrier to bring the subject up, but I'm still upset over something that went on at a party that Stacey was at last week." She paused here and took a deep breath. "I heard that one of the girls in her class was giving oral sex to a few of the boys. Now, I'm not a prude, and I don't think I'm naïve. I know all kinds of things go on with teenagers today that were unheard of when I was a kid. But twelve and thirteen years old! In our community! At a birthday party!"

Everyone at the table wanted to weigh in on the topic:

"It's hard to believe, isn't it? But according to what I've been reading, it's happening everywhere. And with kids who are even younger. And not only at parties. They're doing it in the school bathroom, on the bus, and in the house before their parents come home from work."

"What I find so disturbing is that the kids don't even see it as that big a deal. Oral sex to them is like what a good-night kiss was to us. They don't even think of it as sex. After all, it isn't intercourse, so you're still a virgin. And you can't get pregnant, so they figure it's safe."

"It's *not* safe. That's what's so scary to me. My brother is a doctor, and he told me the kids can get some of the same diseases from oral sex as they can from regular sex—like oral herpes or gonorrhea of the throat. He said that the only protection is a condom. And even that's not 100 percent safe. A boy could have genital warts or lesions on his scrotum, and no condom will help since it doesn't cover that area."

"I feel sick just listening to this. The whole situation is a nightmare. As far as I'm concerned, the only real protection is not doing it at all."

"Yeah, but face it. It's a different world today. And according to what I've been hearing, it's something the girls do for the boys—not the other way around. Some of the girls even do it publicly."

"I've heard that too. Evidently the girl feels pressured to 'perform' in order to be popular. What she doesn't realize is that word gets around, and she gets a reputation for being 'trashy' or a 'slut.'"

"But the boy's reputation gets a boost. He gets bragging rights."

"I worry about both the boys and the girls. How do they feel about themselves afterward—like when they see each other in the hall the next day? And how does having this kind of sex now—and it *is* sex, because if it involves sex organs it's sex—affect their future relationships?"

With each person's comment, Karen grew more visibly agitated. "Okay, okay," she said. "So it's widespread and a lot of kids are into it, but what am I supposed to do about it? I can't ignore it. I know I have to talk to Stacey about what went on at that party. But I don't even know where to begin. The truth is, I'm embarrassed about even bringing up the subject with her."

There was a long pause. People looked at one another blankly and then at me. This wasn't easy. "The one thing I'm sure of," I began, "is what *not* to say: 'Stacey, I know all about what went on at that party you were at last week, and I am shocked and revolted. That is the most disgusting thing I have ever heard! Was there only one girl doing "you know what" to the boys? Are you sure? Did anyone ask you to do it? And did you? Don't lie to me!'

"Instead of giving her your revulsion or the third degree, you'd have a far better chance of having a productive conversation if you tell yourself to keep your tone neutral and your questions general rather than personal. For example, 'Stacey, I just heard something that took me by surprise, and I want to check it out with you. Someone told me that oral sex is going on at kids' parties—even the one you were at last week.'

"Whether she confirms or denies it, you can continue the conversation—again, keeping your tone nonjudgmental: 'Ever since I heard I've been wondering if this is something the girls do because they feel pressured by the boys? Or is it because they think it will make them popular? I've also been wondering what happens if a girl refuses.'

"After Stacey tells you as much as she's comfortable telling, you can express your point of view. But since the subject can be difficult for parents, you might want to take some time beforehand to decide exactly what it is you want to communicate."

"I know what I want to communicate," Karen said ruefully. "I just don't think she could hear it."

Laura looked puzzled. "What couldn't she hear?"

"That I feel it's wrong for one person to use another to satisfy a sexual urge. Or for anyone to 'service' anyone else just to be popular. To me that's demeaning. It's not being respectful to yourself. And that goes for a boy as well as a girl."

"Sounds good to me," Laura said. "Why couldn't you say that to Stacey?"

"I suppose I could." Karen sighed. "But I know my daughter. She'd probably tell me I was being uptight and old-fashioned, that I just didn't 'get it,' and the kids today don't think it's such a big deal. It's just what they do at some parties. So what do I say to that?"

"You can start," I said, "by acknowledging her perspective: 'So to you and a lot of the kids you know it's no big deal.' Then you can go on to share your adult perspective. 'As I see it, oral sex is a very personal, intimate act. Not a party game. Not something you do for fun. And I can't help but wonder if some of the kids who participate don't feel bad about it afterward and wish they hadn't.' No matter what Stacey says after that, you've given her something to think about. At the very least, she knows where her mother stands."

"Right on!" Michael said. "And while you're at it, Stacey should also be told about the health risks. About the STDs kids can get from oral sex. Or any kind of sex, for that matter. She needs to understand that some of the diseases are curable, but some aren't. Some are life-threatening. That's nothing to fool around with."

Laura shook her head. "If it were my kid, she'd have her hands over her ears by now. She could never stand to hear me go on and on about all the horrible diseases she could get."

"But we're the parents!" Michael exclaimed. "Whether the kids like it or not, there's a lot we need to tell them about sex for their own protection."

Laura looked pained. "I know you're right," she acknowledged, "but the truth is, I dread having the 'big talk' with my daughter."

"You're not alone," I said. "The 'big talk' can be embarrassing for both parents and kids. Besides, the subject of sex is too important and too complex to try to tackle in one sitting. Instead, be on the lookout for opportunities that can lead to some 'little' talks. For instance, when you're watching a movie or a TV program together, or listening to the news on the radio, or reading an article in a magazine, you can use what you're seeing or hearing to get a conversation going."

My suggestion sparked an immediate response. Evidently several people were already using this approach with their children. Here, in cartoon form, are some of the examples they shared with the group.

Instead of the One "Big Talk" . . .

The onetime talk about sex can be hard for a parent to deliver and hard for a teenager to listen to.

Look for Opportunities to Have "Small Talks"

While Listening to the Radio

While Reading a Newspaper

While Watching a Sitcom Together

While Driving a Car

Joan raised her hand. "My mother could never, *ever*, have brought up any of these topics with me. She would have died of embarrassment. She did do one thing, though. When I was about twelve, she gave me a book about the 'facts of life.' I pretended I wasn't interested, but I read it from cover to cover. And whenever my girlfriends came over, we'd close the bedroom door, take out 'The Book,' read it again, and giggle over all the pictures."

"What I like about a book," Jim said, "is that it gives the kid a little privacy—a chance to look over the material without someone looking over his shoulder. But no book is going to be a substitute for a parent. Kids want to know what their parents think. What their parents expect of them."

"That's the part that worries me," Laura said. "The 'expect' part. I mean, if you're talking to your kids about sex and giving them books about it with pictures, won't they get the idea that you *expect* them to be having sex and that they've got your permission?"

"Not at all," Michael said. "Not if you make it clear that what you're giving them is information, *not* permission. Besides, it seems to me that if we don't give our kids some basic facts, we could be putting them at risk. If there's anything we believe they should know for their own protection, the only way we can ever be sure they'll know it is to give them the information ourselves."

Michael paused here, searching his mind for an example. "For instance, how many boys know how to use a condom safely— how to actually put it on and take it off? And how many are aware that they need to check the expiration date on the package? Because a dried-out condom is as good as no condom at all."

"Wow," Laura said, "*I* didn't even know that. . . . And I wonder how many girls realize that, no matter what their friends tell them, they *can* get pregnant the first time they have sex— even if they've got their period."

Michael nodded vigorously. "That's just the kind of thing I

mean," he said. "And here's something else. I'll bet it doesn't oc-
cur to most kids that even if they're having sex with a person
who may have had sex with only one other person, that one
other person could have had sex with lots of other people. And
who knows what diseases got passed down along the way!"

Tony frowned. "Everything you all said just now is very important. I mean, you're right. You gotta tell your kids about the
dangers. But shouldn't you also tell them that there's a good part
about sex? That it's normal, natural . . . one of life's pleasures.
Hey, it's how we all got here!"

After the laughter subsided, I said, "Nevertheless, Tony,
those 'normal, natural' feelings can sometimes overwhelm our
kids and play havoc with their judgment. Today's teenagers are
under enormous pressure. Not only from their hormones and
their peers but from a sexualized pop culture that bombards
them with explicit, erotic images on television, in movies, in
music videos, and on the Internet.

"So, yes, it's normal for kids to want to experiment, to act
out what they've seen or heard. And yes, we do want to convey
that sex is 'one of life's pleasures.' But we also need to help our
teenagers set boundaries. We need to share our adult values and
give them some guidelines to hang on to."

"For instance?" Tony said.

I thought a moment. "Well . . . for instance, I think young
people should be told that it's never okay to let anyone pressure
them into doing anything sexual that they're not comfortable
with. They don't have to be unpleasant about it. But they can let
the other person know how they feel. They can simply say, 'I
don't want to do this.'"

"I totally agree," Laura exclaimed. "And anyone who doesn't
respect that isn't a person they should ever go out with again. . . .
And I also think kids should be made to understand that sex isn't
something you do just because you think everybody else is doing

it. You need to do what's right for you. Besides, who knows what's really going on? Maybe some kids *are* having sex, but I'll bet a lot of them aren't and are lying about it."

"And speaking of 'doing what's right for you,'" Joan added, "before kids even think of turning their bodies and souls over to someone else, they ought to ask themselves some serious questions, like, 'Is this a person who really cares about me?' . . . 'Is this someone I can trust?' . . . 'Is this someone I can be myself with?'"

"To me," Karen said, "the main message kids ought to hear from their parents is *'Slow down. There's no need to rush.'* I think it's a big mistake for them to be having sex or hooking up or whatever they call it today, when they're still so young."

"I couldn't agree more!" Joan exclaimed. "These are the years they should be concentrating on their studies and getting involved in different kinds of activities—sports, hobbies, clubs—and doing volunteer work in the community. It's not a time for them to be complicating their lives with sexual relationships. I know they don't want to hear it from us, but still, we should tell them that some things are worth waiting for."

"But there are always going to be some kids who won't wait," Michael pointed out. "And if that's the case, if they're determined to 'go all the way,' they should hear some straight talk from their parents. I'd spell it out for them. I'd tell them they need to have a serious discussion with their prospective partner so that they can decide together just what kind of contraception *each of them* plans to use. Then *both of them* need to check it out with a doctor. My point is, if teenagers think they're grown-up enough to have sex, then they have to be prepared to act like grown-ups. And that means thinking about consequences and taking responsibility."

Jim nodded appreciatively. "Boy, Michael, that really lays it on the line. And of course, everything you said just now goes for all kids—whether they're straight or gay."

There was a sudden silence. Several people looked uneasy.

"I'm glad you added that, Jim," I said. "We do have to recognize the possibility that a young person might be homosexual and that all the precautions Michael recommended just now would apply equally to him or her."

Jim looked hesitant. "I guess the reason I even brought it up," he said, "is because I was thinking of my nephew. He just turned sixteen, and a few weeks ago he confided in me that he's gay. He said the reason he was telling me was because, knowing me, he was pretty sure I'd be okay with it, but he was worried about how his parents would take it. It seems he had been wanting to tell them for a long time but was afraid. Not of his mother's reaction so much. But he didn't know what his father would do if he found out.

"We talked for a long time about the possible fallout, and at one point he said, 'I'm gonna do it, Uncle Jim. I'm gonna tell them.'

"Well, he did. He told them. He said they were both very upset at first. His father wanted him to see a therapist. His mother tried to reassure him. She explained that it wasn't at all unusual for a teenager to feel an occasional attraction to a person of the same sex, but it was probably just a passing thing.

"Then he told her that it wasn't a passing thing, that he'd been having these feelings for a long time now, and he hoped they'd both understand. It must've been very hard for them to hear that, but little by little they seemed to come around. In the end his father was the one who really surprised him. He said that, no matter what, he'd always be their son and that he'd always have their love and support.

"I can tell you that was one relieved young man. And I was

one very relieved uncle. Because if his mother or father had ever turned their back on him over this, I don't know what would have happened. I've read too many stories about kids going into a major depression or even becoming suicidal when their parents reject them because they're gay."

"Your nephew was fortunate," I said. "Coming to terms with a teenager's homosexuality is never easy for any parent. But if we can accept our children for who they truly are, then we've given them a great gift—the strength to be themselves and the courage to begin to deal with the prejudice of the outside world."

Another long silence. "There's something else," Joan said slowly. "Whether our kids are straight or gay, they all need to be made aware that once they decide to add sex to a relationship it's never the same. Everything gets more complicated. All the feelings become more intense. If anything goes wrong, if there's a breakup—which happens all the time with teenagers—it can be devastating for them.

"I remember what went on with my best friend in high school. She was crazy about this boy, let herself get talked into sleeping with him, and after he dumped her for someone else, she went to pieces. Her grades went down, she couldn't eat, sleep, study, or concentrate on anything for the longest time."

Jim threw up his hands. "Well," he announced, "after listening to all this, I'm beginning to think there's a good case to be made for abstinence. Face it, it's the only method that's 100 percent safe. I know someone here is going to tell me that kids are reaching puberty earlier and marrying later and that it's unrealistic to expect them to abstain for so many years, but abstinence doesn't mean they can't go near each other. They can still hold hands, or hug, or kiss, or maybe even go to what we used to call first base. That would be okay . . . I mean, okay for everyone except *my* daughter."

People smiled. Laura looked troubled. "It's easy for us to sit around a table and decide what we should tell our kids they can or can't do. But there's no way we can follow them around twenty-four hours a day. And no matter what we tell them, who says they'll listen?"

"You're right, Laura," I said. "There are no guarantees. No matter what a parent says, some kids will test the limits and some will go beyond the limits. Nevertheless, all the skills you've been putting into practice these past few months make it far more likely that your kids *will* be able to listen to you. But even more important, they'll have the confidence to listen to themselves and set their own limits."

"From your mouth to God's ears!" Tony called out. "I sure as hell hope that what you said just now applies to drugs too, because I'm getting a bad feeling about some of the kids my son is starting to hang out with. They don't have the greatest reputation—one of them was suspended for getting high in school—and I don't want my boy influenced by him. I mean, if they're trying to get him to use drugs, I want to know what I can do to head them off. Like what should I say to him?"

"What would you like to say?" I asked.

"What my father said to me."

"What was that?"

"That he'd break every bone in my body if he ever caught me using drugs."

"Did that stop you?"

"No. I just made sure he never caught me."

I laughed. "So at least now you know what not to do."

Laura jumped in. "How about if you tell him, 'Listen, if anyone tries to talk you into doing drugs, just say *no*.' "

Tony gave me a what-do-you-think look.

"The problem with that approach," I said, "is that by itself it's not enough. Kids need to hear more than a simple 'just say no.' They're under enormous pressure today to just say yes. The combination of all the messages in the pop culture and the easy availability of drugs and the urging of their peers can be hard to resist: 'You gotta try this' . . . 'Trust me, you'll like it' . . . 'This stuff is really great' . . . 'It feels sooo good!' . . . 'Helps you relax' . . . 'Come on, don't be a wimp.'

"And as if that weren't enough, scientists are now telling us that although a teenager may appear physically mature, his brain is still in the process of being formed. The part that controls impulses and exercises judgment is one of the very last areas of the brain to develop."

"That's so scary," Laura said.

"Yes, it is," I agreed, "but the good news is that you all have more power than you realize. Your kids care deeply about what you think. They may not always show it, but your values and convictions are very important to them and can be the determining factor in their decision to either use or avoid drugs and alcohol. For example, Tony, you can tell your son, 'I sure hope your friend isn't into drugs anymore. He's a nice kid, and I hate to think of him messing up his future because of what he's putting into his body today.'

"And it's not only our words that can keep our children from risky behavior, it's also what we model. It's what our kids see us do or not do that speaks volumes to them."

"Now that hits home," Joan commented. "My father once grounded me because he found out I had one little drink at a party. But I used to see him every night with his cocktail before dinner and beer with dinner, so I figured if it was okay for him, it was okay for me."

"At least your father had an idea about what was going on with you," Laura said, "and was trying to be responsible. A lot of parents today are clueless. They figure that if their kid *seems* to be doing everything right, then everything is right. But you can't ever really be sure. I read an article recently about these teenagers from a wealthy community. They were on the honor roll, on all the teams, and every weekend they were binge drinking. And the parents had no idea until a few of them ended up in the hospital and one of them nearly died.

"That story is a wakeup call," I said. "Binge drinking goes on in many communities today. It's a major concern for parents, especially since we now know that teen drinking is more dangerous than we previously thought. All the recent studies show that the adolescent brain is in a critical stage of development. Alcohol destroys brain cells, causes neurological damage, memory loss, learning problems, and puts a youngster's overall health at risk. There's also new evidence that the earlier kids start drinking, the greater the chance of their becoming alcoholics as adults."

"Oh great!" Tony said. "Now that we know all that, how do we get it into the heads of our dopey kids? They don't think anything could ever happen to them. They'll go to a party and dare one another to see who can drink the most before throwing up or passing out."

"Which is why," I said, "we need to be very clear and very specific when we tell our children, *'Binge drinking can kill you. Putting a large amount of alcohol into your body at any one time can lead to alcohol poisoning. And alcohol poisoning can lead to coma or death. That's a medical fact.'*"

Joan put her hands to her head. "This is too much for me," she groaned. "Alcohol by itself is bad enough, but everything I've been reading says that teenagers who do a lot of drinking are also into doing drugs. And there's so much new stuff out there that I never even heard of before. It's not just pot or crack or LSD anymore. Now there's ecstasy, and . . ."

People were quick to add to Joan's list: ". . . and roofies, the date rape drug."

"And something called Ketamine, or 'Special K.'"

"And how about methamphetamines? That's supposed to be even more addictive than cocaine."

"I heard about something new the kids inhale to get high. It's called poppers or liquid gold."

"Boy," Tony said, shaking his head, "there's a helluva lot to know, isn't there."

"It can seem overwhelming," I said, "but the information is all out there—in books, in magazines, and on the Internet. You can call a substance abuse hotline and ask for their current pamphlets. You can talk to other parents in your community and find out what they know. And while you're at it, you can ask your son what he knows about what the kids in his school are using today."

"Well," Tony said, "looks like I've got my work cut out for me."

"All parents of teenagers," I said, "have their work cut out for them. We all need to make it clear to our kids that their mothers and fathers are informed, involved, ready to do whatever it takes to protect them.

"And once again, a onetime lecture won't do the job. Kids need to hear your thoughts about drugs in different ways and at different times. They need to feel comfortable enough to ask you questions, to answer your questions, and to explore their own thoughts and feelings.

"So . . . on to our final challenge! How can we take advantage of a small opportunity that might present itself in the course of a day to engage our children in a dialogue about drugs? What kinds of conversations can we imagine having with our teenagers?"

After much back and forth, the group envisioned the following scenarios.

Take Advantage of Small Opportunities to Talk About Drugs

Reading a Newspaper

Watching a Commercial

Commenting on Something You Notice

Looking at a Magazine

Setting an Example

Commenting on a Radio Program

As we were discussing our last example, Laura's hand shot up. "So far all we've been talking about is how to steer our kids away from using drugs. But what if a kid is already using stuff? I mean, what if it's too late?"

"It's never too late to exercise your power as a parent," I said. "Even if it's a onetime only 'experiment,' it can't be ignored. You need to confront your teenager, review the risks, and reaffirm your values and expectations.

"If, however, you suspect that your teenager is already using drugs with some frequency, if you notice changes in behavior, grades, appearance, attitude, friends, sleeping patterns, or eating habits, then it's time to take action: Let your child know what you've observed. Listen to his or her side of the story. Learn whatever you can about what's really going on. Call a local or national drug abuse program for additional information. Consult with your doctor. Investigate whatever services are available in your community that can offer professional counseling and treatment. In other words, get help. You can't do it alone."

"I hope I never have to do it at all." Laura sighed. "Maybe I'll get lucky and my kids will turn out just great."

"You have more than luck to depend upon, Laura," I said. "You've got skills. And even more important, you understand the attitude that gives heart to the skills. All of you do. Over these past few months you've made many changes in the way you communicate with your children. And all of these changes—both large and small—can make a profound difference in your relationship with them.

"By being responsive to your teenagers' feelings, by working out problems together, by encouraging them to reach for their goals and realize their dreams, you let your kids know every day how much you respect and love and value them. And young people who feel valued by their parents are more likely to value themselves, more likely to make responsible choices, less likely to get involved in behavior that would work against their own best interests or jeopardize their future."

Silence. It had been a long session, yet everyone seemed reluctant to leave.

"I'm going to miss these classes." Laura sighed. "Not just for the skills but for all the support I've gotten from everyone here." Her eyes welled up. "And I'm going to miss hearing about everybody's kids."

Karen hugged her. Michael did too.

"What I'll miss most," Joan said, "is knowing I have people I can talk to if a problem comes up."

"And as we all well know," Jim commented ruefully, "with teenagers there are always going to be new problems. That's why it's been great to have a place to go where you can get some feedback from people who are in the same boat."

"Hey," Tony said, "who says we have to quit? How about we keep on meeting—not every week maybe, but like every month or two?"

Tony's suggestion was met with an immediate, enthusiastic response.

Everyone looked at me expectantly.

I thought for a moment. What these parents wished for themselves was what I wished for all parents of teenagers—an ongoing support system. The relief of no longer feeling isolated. The comfort of being able to unburden yourself to people you know will understand. The hope that springs from exchanging ideas and seeing new possibilities. The pleasure of sharing small triumphs with one another.

"If that's what you all want," I said to the group, "keep me posted. I'll be there."

Sex and Drugs

Instead of One Big Lecture ("I know you think you know all about sex and drugs, but I think it's time we had a talk")

LOOK FOR SMALL OPPORTUNITIES TO GET A CONVERSATION GOING

Listening to the radio: "Do you think what that psychologist said just now is right? Do kids have a hard time refusing drugs because they don't want to look geeky or lose friends?"

Watching television: "So, according to this commercial, all a girl has to do to get a guy interested in her is wear the right color lip gloss."

Reading a magazine: "What do you think of this? It says here, 'Sometimes kids take drugs just to feel good. But then they have to use drugs—just to feel normal.'"

Watching a movie: "Did that last scene seem realistic? Would two teenagers who just met jump into bed together?"

Reading a newspaper: "When you have time, take a look at this article about teens and binge-drinking. I'd be interested in your reaction."

Listening to music: "How do you feel about these lyrics? Do you think they could affect the way guys treat girls?"

Next Time We Meet . . .

In the days that followed I found my thoughts returning to the group again and again.

We had been on a long journey together. Different people had started out with different hopes, different fears, and different destinations in mind. Yet no matter what their original reasons for coming to the workshop meetings, they all had the satisfaction of seeing not only that their new skills improved their relationships with their teenagers, but that their teenagers were behaving more responsibly. Accomplishments we could all feel good about!

Still, I was glad we'd be meeting again. It would give me a chance to share with the parents what had been welling up within me with increasing clarity—the larger view of what our work together had been about.

Next time I'll tell them that if it is indeed true that "children learn what they live," then what their children had been living and learning over these past few months were the most basic principles of caring communication. Every day, in the push and pull of family life, their teenagers were learning that:

- **Feelings matter.** Not just your own, but those of people with whom you disagree.
- **Civility matters.** Anger can be expressed without insult.
- **Words matter.** What you choose to say can cause resentment or generate goodwill.
- **Punishment has no place in a caring relationship.** We're all people in process—capable of making mistakes and capable of facing our mistakes and making amends.
- **Our differences needn't defeat us.** Problems that seem insoluble can yield to respectful listening, creativity, and persistence.
- **We all need to feel valued.** Not only for who we are now, but for who we can become.

Next time we meet, I'll tell the parents that each day offers new opportunities. Each day gives them a chance to demonstrate the attitude and language that can serve their teenagers in the present moment and in all the years ahead.

Our children are our gift to tomorrow. What they experience in our homes today will empower them to bring to the world they inherit the ways that affirm the dignity and humanity of all people.

That's what I'll tell the parents—next time.

Additional Reading
That May Be Helpful

Elkind, David, PhD. *Parenting Your Teenager in the 1990s: Practical Information and Advice About Adolescent Development and Contemporary Issues*. Cambridge, MA: Modern Learning Press, 1993. Dr. Elkind addresses many of the issues that continue to confront parents of teenagers a decade later. He offers insights and advice in a supportive, readable manner.

Faber, Adele, and Elaine Mazlish. *How to Talk So Kids Will Listen and Listen So Kids Will Talk,* revised edition. New York: HarperCollins, 2004. Recommended for two reasons:

1. The chapter on autonomy—how to help a child become a separate, independent individual who can one day function on his own—is especially relevant during the teen years.

2. The chapter on how to free a child from being trapped in a role (for example, lazy, complainer, princess, disorganized) applies to teenagers as well. It's never too late to help a young person see himself differently and realize his potential.

————. *How to Talk So Kids Can Learn: At Home and in School*. New York: Rawson Associates, 1995. Describes the kind of communication that motivates students to think, learn, persist, and believe in themselves.

Giannetti, Charlene, and Margaret Sagarese. *The Roller-Coaster Years: Raising Your Child Through the Maddening Yet Magical Middle School Years*. New York: Broadway Books, 1997. A lively, practical book that deals with the wide range of issues affecting most middle-schoolers and their parents.

Hersch, Patricia. *A Tribe Apart: A Journey into the Heart of American Adolescence*. New York: Ballantine Books, 1998. A gifted journalist takes you deep inside the world of eight very different teenagers and reveals the passions and pressures that shape their personality and character during their adolescent years.

Lopez, Ralph, MD. *The Teen Health Book: A Parents' Guide to Adolescent Health and Well-being*. New York: W. W. Norton & Co., 2002. An excellent resource. Written in a clear and friendly style, it addresses both the physical and emotional concerns of teenagers.

McGraw, Jay. *Closing the Gap: A Strategy for Bringing Parents and Teens Together*. New York: Fireside/Simon & Schuster, 2001. Advice to both parents and teens from the personal perspective of a young college student.

Pipher, Mary, PhD. *Reviving Ophelia: Saving the Lives of Adolescent Girls*. New York: Ballantine Books, 1995. A look at the harm done to our daughters by the current culture, along with sensible strategies for how to help them.

Pollack, William, PhD. *Real Boys: Rescuing Our Sons from the Myths of Boyhood*. New York: Owl Books, Henry Holt and Company, 1999. A logical companion to *Reviving Ophelia, Real Boys* makes clear how our gender stereotypes harm our sons and offers a wealth of caring alternatives.

Richardson, Justin, MD, and Schuster, Mark A., MD, PhD. *Everything You Never Wanted Your Kids to Know About Sex (But Were Afraid They'd Ask): The Secrets to Surviving Your Child's Sexual Development from Birth to the Teens*. New York: Three

Rivers Press, 2003. The title says it all. Sound, sensible advice on dealing with a tough topic.

Sheras, Peter, PhD, with Sherill Tippins. *Your Child: Bully or Victim? Understanding and Ending Schoolyard Tyranny*. New York: Fireside/Simon & Schuster, 2002. A thoughtful exploration of the causes and effects of bullying and suggestions for how to deal with it.

Taffel, Dr. Ron, with Melinda Blau. *The Second Family: Reckoning with Adolescent Power*. New York: St. Martin's Press, 2001. Dr. Taffel takes an unflinching look at how peers and the current pop culture can push parents to the sidelines of their teenagers' lives. He recommends a variety of ways to renew and strengthen the connection between the generations.

Walsh, David, PhD. *Why Do They Act That Way?: A Survival Guide to the Adolescent Brain for You and Your Teen*. New York: Free Press, 2004. Dr. Walsh draws upon the latest research about the adolescent brain as well as his own extensive experience with troubled teens to give parents valuable insights, information, and guidelines.

To Learn More . . .

If you are interested in having a chance to discuss and practice the communication skills in this book with others, please visit www.fabermazlish.com. There you'll find information about:

- Group workshops for parents and professionals
- Individual workshops
- Books for parents and professionals
- Books for kids
- Audio- and videotapes
- Creative solutions to parenting problems
- Adele and Elaine's newsletter, the *Faber/Mazlish Forum*
- And much more!

Or you may request a brochure by sending a self-addressed, stamped business envelope to:

Faber/Mazlish Workshops, LLC
PO Box 64
Albertson, NY 10507

Index

BOOKS BY ADELE FABER & ELAINE MAZLISH

HOW TO TALK SO TEENS WILL LISTEN & LISTEN SO TEENS WILL TALK

ISBN 0-06-074125-2 (hardcover)

Filled with straightforward advice and sure to appeal to both parents and teens, this all-new volume offers both innovative and proven techniques to build the foundation for lasting relationships. It gives parents the tools to help their children safely navigate the often stormy years of adolescence.

HOW TO TALK SO KIDS WILL LISTEN & LISTEN SO KIDS WILL TALK

ISBN 0-380-81196-0 (paperback)

Here is the bestselling book that will give you the know-how you need to be effective with your children. Enthusiastically praised by parents and professionals around the world, the down-to-earth, respectful approach of Faber and Mazlish makes relationships with children of all ages less stressful and more rewarding.

SIBLINGS WITHOUT RIVALRY
How to Help Your Children Live Together So You Can Live Too

ISBN 0-380-79900-6 (paperback)

Guides the way to family peace and tranquillity with humor and compassion for both parents and children. Illustrated, action-oriented, and easy to understand, it's packed with sensitive yet sensible ways to turn quarreling siblings and frustrated parents into an open, communicative family.

LIBERATED PARENTS, LIBERATED CHILDREN
Your Guide to a Happier Family

ISBN 0-380-71134-6 (paperback)

Wisdom, humor, and practical advice are the hallmarks of this indispensable book that demonstrates the kind of communication that builds self-esteem, inspires confidence, encourages responsibility, and makes a major contribution to the stability of today's family.